ORPHANS

To:
John L. Carr

Ollie Kirby

9-01-01

ORPHANS

*The Journey of
the Six Reuter Children*

Ollie Kirby

Copyright © 1999 by Ollie Kirby.

Library of Congress Number: 99-91666
ISBN #:   Hardcover   0-7388-1178-5
           Softcover   0-7388-1179-3

All rights reserved. No part of this book may be reproduced or transmitted in any form or by any means, electronic or mechanical, including photocopying, recording, or by any information storage and retrieval system, without permission in writing from the copyright owner.

This is a work of fiction. Names, characters, places and incidents either are the product of the author's imagination or are used fictitiously, and any resemblance to any actual persons, living or dead, events, or locales is entirely coincidental.

This book was printed in the United States of America.

To order additional copies of this book, contact:
Xlibris Corporation
1-888-7-XLIBRIS
www.Xlibris.com
Orders@Xlibris.com

CONTENTS

PREFACE
    PRE-SETTLER DAYS 9

CHAPTER 1
    SEDRO WOOLLEY, WASHINGTON 1893 19

CHAPTER 2
    THREE LAKES, WASHINGTON 1900 35

CHAPTER 3
    1909 42

CHAPTER 4
    RETURN TO SEDRO WOOLLEY 1916 55

CHAPTER 5
    ROSE & JANET 1918 67

CHAPTER 6
    WAR AND DEPRESSION 1919 86

CHAPTER 7
    HOMESTEAD LIFE 1922 111

CHAPTER 8
    DENVER 1927 122

CHAPTER 9
    THE GREAT DUST BOWL 1930 136

CHAPTER 10
    WORLD WAR II 1940 149

CHAPTER 11
    EMPTY NEST 1950 199

CHAPTER 12
    1960 204

I dedicate this book to my children,

*my brothers and sister
who have helped me put some of the events together,*

*my cousins
who have been so kind to fill me in on their memories,*

*and
my editor Jane Allbritton
who kept me on track to finish this story.*

PREFACE

PRE-SETTLER DAYS

Sedro in Washington Territory was actually born in 1889. The town that the Gillis Brothers (featured in this book) found in the 1890s was rough-hewn as most of the Western frontier villages were, hacked and fashioned from cedar and fir. Folks who lived here in 1889 worked from dawn to dusk in the woods or on the Skagit River, and Sunday was their day off, if they were lucky. If they really got lucky, they hoisted their main squeeze up on top of a cedar stump and shook their bones to a Virginia Reel on Saturday night. According to June Burn, a columnist for the Bellingham Herald in the early 1930s, saloons in old Sedro stood on stilts along the shore. Survivors from that pioneer era told her that more than one logger slept overnight wherever he toppled over into the mud.

    Actually the two surviving photos from that period show that the main street was about 100 yards from the shore, but the streets were muddy eight months out of the year. Dancing women occasionally entertained in the ruggedgyp joints, but hard-core drinking was the most common floorshow. Skagit pioneers assumed that rain was their destiny and they celebrated the infrequent arrival of the sun. To make do on misty days they invented sunbeams in their minds. Charles Easton, founder of the fine bookstore in Mount Vernon, put it best in a 1969 Puget Soundings article. "Pioneers came knowing full well the problems they would face. They accepted accidents, sickness amd death philosophically. They were convinced that hard, backbreaking work would in time lead to an easier, better life." If a family was even a moderately good hunter or fisher, they would not go hungry on this fruitful land.

The river didn't spawn many famous people, but it sure housed some great ones. History writers in the county have long given short shrift to the early Sedro-Woolley events. For a short period from 1889-1890, Sedro was one of the most famous towns on the frontier and financiers from all over the country were placing bets on the town's future. Many west-county residents assume that we are all pinheads as a result of intermarriage. The Seattle Times two years ago even printed an insulting application for prospective residents, but we laughed along with everyone else. That is how the pioneers would have reacted. The truth is that upriver towns share a historical treasury. George Washington did not sleep here, but Mortimer Cook did. There was no high noon, but J. J. Donovan did race through a blizzard to deliver a choo-choo train for a Christmas present to Sedro in1889. One-eyed James J. Hill of Great Northern fame met Jesus Christ here, and Norman Kelley and Duke Frederick George of Bavaria (and later of Duke's Hill)drank champagne and scotch respectively until they croaked. From the beginning of the white man era, this area has attracted many men and women who were either reckless or bewildered, but most of them shared a trait that was important to the frontier: they possessed a skill or spirit that could be woven into the community at large. If they did not fit in, they just moved on to another town or deeper into the wilderness. In today's parlance, they were risk takers.

The whole west coast of America and Canada was defined by major gold rushes, the first in 1849 at Sutter's mill in California, then in 1858 on the Fraser River in British Columbia, and finally in 1897-98 in Alaska. Most of our pioneers moved to California or traveled through that state before they came here.Sedro-Woolley was born 23 miles up the Skagit River and 63 miles north of Seattle because gold miners and trappers told people back home about gigantic Douglas fir, Western hemlock and Western red cedar trees, which they claimed were as big around as bedrooms. In fact, some of the cedar stumps really were used as bedrooms. Cedar trees thrived wherever water stood for long periods; firs sank their roots on riverbanks. The glacier-fed Skagit River meandered allover the valley for thousands of years, so loggers found trees standing for miles north and south of the ancient riverbed that flowed nearly parallel to latitude 48o30' north. A Bellingham Herald article in 1906 describes one fir in Sedro that was 54 feet in circumference and 328 feet high, although most of those ancient trees soared a mere 200-225 feet [en] Imagine for a moment the day the first hearty tree climber shinnied up a fir or cedar. At the top of one, he saw a sea of treetops with a handful reaching up more than 300 feet towards the sky, longer than a football field. Although gold petered out for miners by the mid-1880s, as did the trappers' market for beaver pelts years before, trees seemed inexhaustible. Spotted owls had plenty of room to roam back then.

Art Robinson, an old Tarheel (North Carolina) logger and cousin of the famous Pinky Robinson, took my family out to a first-growth forest back in the early '50s and showed us some of the giant trees that predated the Protestant Reformation of the 16th century. Describing the sensation he felt when one of the firs crashed to the forest floor, he asked me to imagine my school bus dropping from the top of the tree. "It's like one of them San Francisco earthquakes every time," he drawled. The ice age formed the Skagit

The Skagit River rises about a hundred miles northeast of here in British Columbia, Canada. From there it turns southeast, then south through the North Cascades mountain range and finally almost due west down the Skagit Valley. Geologists explain that, during the most recent Ice Age about 10-15,000 years ago, a massive continental ice sheet delimited the Skagit. One lobe progressed south from the Fraser River valley and another grew east from what is now Puget Sound. In between, the Skagit resulted largely from stream erosion between these two lobes as they melted. The Skagit carries the largest volume of water of any river between the Fraser in southern British Columbia and the Columbia, which forms the border between parts of Washington and Oregon states.

Nearly 3,500 streams and other rivers feed into it before the river reaches the Puget Sound near LaConner. It is the largest river to feed into Puget Sound. The Skagit River channel changed size and shape countless times since the last Ice Age, adjusting to glacial melt and volcanic flow. The Skagit valley is where the river levels out west of a narrow gorge by present-day Concrete. For more than 50 miles above here, before the hydroelectric dams were built earlier this century, the river rushed through gorges and channels, picking up steam. At Rockport it is joined by the Sauk River, which is fed in turn just a few miles southeast by the Suiattle. At the site that became Concrete, it was widened again by the Baker River. Volcanoes, floods and log jams

European exploration of what is now northwest Washington dates from the 16th Century, but the area was really first charted in depth in June 1792 by English Capt. George Vancouver, from his ship Discovery. The famed British sailing captain and explorer was the first European to explore the waters of San Juan de Fuca. South of the island that Vancouver named for himself, he discovered an inland sea, which he named for one of his officers, Lieutenant Peter Puget. He named a bay on the eastern shore of Puget Sound for Sir William Bellingham, keeper of the British Navy storekeeper's accounts back in England. That bay is located just south of where another large river (named for the Nooksack tribe) empties into the sound. About 60 years later, Henry Roeder chose that bay as the site for his sawmill and the village of Whatcom, which is now part of the town of Bellingham.

Vancouver named the dominant mountain east of Bellingham, Mount Baker, for another ship's officer, Lieutenant Joseph Baker. Newcomers have used its symmetrical snowy peaks for navigation the last 150 years. Indians told Vancouver's crew about occasional fiery volcanic eruptions on the mountain. Later that same year, a Spanish explorer's ship ran aground in Bellingham Bay and the crew witnessed an eruption on Mount Baker. The sight alarmed the captain so much that he sailed the ship away as soon as possible. In 1880, Indians told white Sedro settlers Joseph Hart and

Harry Devin about volcanic lava that whooshed south from Mount Baker down the Baker River and pushed logs, boulders and soil into the Skagit River. The debris washed downstream to the present site of Mount Vernon, forming two massive logjams that became a major impediment to exploration of the Skagit. After conversations with Larry Kunzler, a Skagit County flood-control expert, we have hypothesized that an eruption, possibly in 1792 may have washed debris down the Skagit that formed the base for the logjams that limited exploration of the Skagit until the 1880s. We know from first-hand accounts that firs were growing out of these jams of timber to a height of 90 feet and firs grow about a foot per year.

The logjams blocked all but the heartiest pioneers from exploring upriver in the 1850s through '70s. The Skagit River channel formed an "S" above and below Mount Vernon, which was about two miles long. The northern bend formed where the town of Avon was soon platted, and the southern bend was located where Edgewater Park now stands in west Mount Vernon. The lower logjam was at least a century old, a conglomeration of silt, vegetation and driftwood about half-mile long. The upper jam began a half-mile north of the lower one and was about a mile long. Sediment had lodged so thick on both jams that each one sprouted growth of brush and large trees that approached 100 feet. The logjams were cleared enough for navigation by 1878 and two bachelors from England settled the future site of Sedro-Woolley. David Batey and Joseph Hart took a steamboat from San Francisco to Seattle, where they boarded another steamboat LaConner. They bought an old salt chuck (sea)canoe in LaConner and paddled down the sound to the north fork of the Skagit River. From there they poled upstream to the two log jams where settlers had hacked a narrow channel. But the current was so swift that the newcomers were forced to portage their belongings on a blazed trail around the obstructions. They then returned to skid their canoe around the same route. Indians made good money for their skills at portaging. The entire process took as long as three days, depending on the weather. After a short visit with a minister who tended his flock from the Sound to the Cascades, Batey and Hart poled upriver after the minister advised them how to navigate and avoid the nasty snags in the fast flowing current. They found a natural landing located just west of future Sedro that we now call Hart's Island, a horseshoe-shaped sandbar where Indians camped for centuries.

In those early months they were alone and many times that year they were destitute. The outside world was still reeling from the 1873 financial panic, but they were living on their own Walden Pond, independent from urban centers. The only sounds they heard were those of nature—the crashing river, chattering birds, wind blowing through the leaves, and the screams of wild animals, including bears, cougars and mountain lions. Eliza Van Fleet later wrote that the men learned to subsist like the Skagit Indians who camped on the island. Indians taught them how to fish for salmon and steelhead. The bachelor settlers relished the Indians' bullhead (fish) stews and they learned to make sauces from the wild crabapples and currants they found growing near the riverbank. Indians taught them to cut out the acorn gland in a bear's knees that spoiled the taste of meat. Initially they did not even have nails for building a cabin. They chopped cedar trees and split lumber to build a shack out of poles, rough boards and blankets. When the wind blew they had to run out and stand on both sides of their lean-to and hold the pieces together by hand until the wind subsided. They were joined by two other bachelors from England that fall. For the next six years these four men and two handfuls of other hearty settlers began slowly cutting the abundant timber along the shoreline.

Everyone along the river was dependent on it alone for transportation. The dense forest and the muddy soil many months of the year conspired to discourage travel overland so freight, passengers and products from settlers farms were all carried on either Indian canoes hewed out of cedar or small sternwheeler steamboats. The sternwheeler was preferred on the river because it had a very shallow draft and could shove up onto the low sandy banks. As more settlers and loggers moved to the area, those with foresight realized that a railroad would be needed to transport the logs from trees rising up to 300 feet and more. Mortimer Cook founds Sedro

In 1884 the former mayor of Santa Barbara, California bought timber rights on acreage that extended from Hart and Batey's original site up and over the low foothills north of the river. Mortimer Cook had visited this area during the short-lived 1858 gold rush on the Fraser River in British Columbia. Four years later he founded a town on the Thompson river nearby there, which he called Cook's Ferry. When he came back in 1884 he laid out plans for a mill which he built on the north shore of the river in 1885. It was the first shingle mill of its kind, incorporating a drying kiln that reduced the weight of the wet cedar shingles so that they could be shipped to markets in California and the East.

The genesis for the town, however, was due to the discovery in the late 1870s of coal veins that extended southeast from similar deposits around the Washington-British Columbia border. The most pronounced vein that was easiest to mine lay about six miles northeast of the mill and general store that Cook built on the river. In 1888 a railroad promoter named Nelson Bennett came to the area and bought the mineral rights and dreamed up a railroad to transport it to ships on the Puget Sound. In just one year's time Bennett constructed the first standard gauge railroad north of Seattle, stretching from the river and coal mines to Bellingham Bay. The investment in the railroad also attracted Eastern investment capital to clear and build the town of Sedro in 1889. That town was soon eclipsed, however, after an eastern promoter named P.A. Woolley purchased land a mile northwest in 1890. Woolley had the foresight to realize that three railroads would soon cross at that point, so he started his own company town for his own sawmill, all of which he named after himself.

The decade of the '90s started with a roar as the two towns competed for business connected with the three railroad routes, the coal mine, the lumber mills and the farms that were sprouting up on the logged-off lands. Then the national financial panic of 1893 pulled the rug out from underneath the two towns. They did not recover until 1898-99 as a result of another gold rush, this time the bonanza of them all, in the Klondike region of Alaska. By the time that the Gillis Brothers of this book were establishing their newspaper, the twin towns were roaring full speed, riding the back of a second boom economy.

After nearly ten years of fighting each other, the two towns merged in December 1898 and became Sedro-Woolley. At the turn of the century the town dominated the commerce of the county and attracted both upwardly mobile, young middle-class entrepreneurs and settler families. Some of the Gillis brothers developed the new Murdock Junction addition on the eastern border of the old town of Woolley. Other Gillis brothers published the Skagit County Times, forerunner of the present Courier-Times.

The Cokedale Mines provided one of the most consistent payrolls of the area as 50 beehive coke ovens were built to process the coal that was highly valued in steel making. Steam "donkeys" were dotting all the low foothills of the Cascades as logging moved up and away from the rivers. Logging was still backbreaking work and dependent on strong young men and teams of oxen that were used to drag the logs on skid roads down to the Skagit River. The donkeys powered long cables that drug the logs from one point to another. At the river the logs were boomed together and pushed downriver to log yards at Riverside in Mount Vernon. At one time there were 17 shingle mills within just a few-mile radius of Sedro-Woolley and hundreds of men worked 6 or 6 1/2 days weeks, 12 hours a day.

Men still outnumbered women in the area by a ratio of 2 to 1 as the century began. In the early days, when Caucasian women were scarce, loggers and farmers took squaws as wives. These young girls from the various Skagit Indian bands were called Klootchman and were expected to literally keep the home fires burning on pre-emption claims. Early settlers were able to claim up to 160 acres apiece of government land at a cost of $1.25 per acre. As women began braving the trip from back east or California, the klootchmen were usually unceremoniously sent back to the reservation near LaConner, but some stayed on the family farms, becoming babysitters for the children of the new wives.

Population surged in the new town in the first decade of the century, growing rapidly past 1,500. Telephones were installed in 1899, originally from the office of the Skagit County Times. Soon thereafter electric power was installed beginning in 1902, water was piped in from springs in the hills south of the river and a sewer system was dug underneath the main parts of town throughout the decade.

By 1906 Sedro-Woolley was a bustling town with most of the amenities that were available in Seattle. Over the next six years real wealth doubled and tripled as two key developments occurred. First, a second state mental hospital was built 3 miles northeast of town. A vast 1,200 acre campus was laid out and designed to be self sustaining, with its own power plant, dairy, and greenhouse, and crews of inmates who performed almost all the necessary jobs under close supervision. Then in 1912 an eastern development company extended an interurban railway to Sedro-Woolley, tying the town to the outside world and connecting to a system from Seattle and Bellingham. This also opened up the river to hydroelectric development by the same company and over the next few decades they would build dams that would power much of the western part of Washington state. The area continued to boom through World War I and attracted an entirely new population of loggers, farmers and young businessman who built the town that we know today. Noel V. Bourasaw

For further information about this rich Skagit River district, you can write to: Skagit River Journal, 810 Central Ave., Sedro-Woolley, WA 98284, 360-855-1805. Email: *nbourasaw@netscape.net*

Bourasaw is preparing a book on the area: "From Bug to the Bughouse, the first 50 years of Sedro-Woolley and the Upper Skagit River. Please inquire for details.

CHAPTER I

SEDRO WOOLLEY, WASHINGTON 1893

I was a little nervous as I walked up the steps to Aunt Josephine's freshly painted cottage. At ninety she was still pretty spry. She greeted me at the door and as I walked into her parlor, there were two overstuffed sofas facing each other. Each sofa had a beautiful afghan draped over it. She didn't hesitate to tell me that she made the afghans and she was working on another for me to take when my visit was over.

"I am so glad I have this chance to visit you, I have had so many questions about my family and no one to ask,"

We chatted over a cup of tea, and after awhile she started talking about the Gillis family.

"Tell me more, Aunt Josephine, what happened to Aunt Rosalie, did she die?" I asked.

"Oh, my no, she had to have a kidney removed. Janette brought her home as soon as she was able to travel and she spent the rest of the summer getting her strength back."

"Did my Grandma Lydia marry the lumberman?" I asked

"Not right away, he courted Lydia all summer and wrote her love letters. In December he asked Janette if he could marry her daughter," explained Josephine. "And what did Grandma Gillis say to him?" I asked eagerly.

"She said she would have to talk it over with Mr. Gillis and they would give him an answer later," said Josephine.

Letter from Anna Janet Gillis to J.J. Reuter in answer to his request for her daughter's hand in marriage. Reprinted from the original letter.

Sedro
Dec. 13th 1893

Mr. J.J. Reuter
My Dear Friend,

 In answer to your favor of the 11th asking for my approval of the union of yourself and Lydia Martella. I feel quite sure that you have so far shown by your gentlemanly actions and loving care of her to have won for yourself the love of my family all have thought highly of you. And as for myself, I am sure I could not ask for her a more loving companion in life. You remember that if you persuade her to become your truist it will be a few months. That is much more preferable to me as she is quite young yet and I think you may have quite a pleasant engagement. I am sure you will always have my love and best wishes through life. I did not mention this to Mr. G. as I thought there was ample time for that. Now I need not remind you that this is a weary world and there will be little cares but with pure love they will be lighter. So be true to your vows and with God blessing you will be happy.

Ever your true friend,
Mrs. Janet Gillis

"What did Grandpa John say when Grandma told him that this man wanted to marry his daughter?" I asked.

"Even though Janette was in charge of the household, John had the final say in important decisions. She didn't tell him right away," said Josephine.

"When did they finally marry?" I prodded.

"Well, Joseph, your grandfather, finally won over Janette and John and they consented to the marriage. It seems like everyone chose the month of June to get married, so, they had months to plan the wedding and make all the gowns. My, we were all put to work helping to plan this wedding. Lydia was thrilled, she wanted her dress to be perfect, so she was very fussy about getting started on it right away."

"What was my grandfather like?" I asked.

"He was a serious man, but he liked to gamble, he would spend time at the saloon on occasion. Sometimes Albert and Walter would join him. They wanted to get to know Joseph better. John and Janette didn't know this side of their new son-in-law to be," said Josephine.

"How did you know this went on?" I asked.

"I overheard Walter and Albert talking on the porch while everyone was in the house busy with the wedding plans.

Albert and I hadn't been married very long ourselves, and I was taking them some fresh lemonade when I heard their conversation," said Josephine.

Sedro Jan. 22, 1894
8:05 P.M.

My Dear Martella,
You cannot imagine how glad I was to see you down here this afternoon. And your looking so charming although you were not feeling well you did not show it in your action or in your looks for you were just as pretty as you could be. It was very good of you to come, as you knowed that it would please your Joe. Soon dearest, Mr. C. will come back and he will mostly go for the mail and then I can not see you only at times when you come down or if I by chance go for the mail. Of Sunday evening if he is here, I will be with you, during the week I can not promise to be with you any evening as he delights in keeping me in every evening that he can. At times he would give almost anything if he could keep me in the store or at the house Sunday night too, but that he will never accomplish when he is at home. Still he has always said "alright" when I would tell him that I was going out a while and in everything in regard to business work and talk he has always treated me more like a son than as a clerk. And for that I will always respect him and I will even let my darling go to church without me in order to please him. When he is not here as I done last night. But after all I enjoyed that

walk and my stay at your house dearest as well as I ever injoyed anything in my life, and that is saying a whole lot. You treat me so well dearest that I cannot myself doubly repaid for all that I have been able to do for you, dear one; And as long as I can so live that my darling will not regret having given me her pure innocent and youthful love. Just so long dearest my happiness is as near complete as it can be on earth. But should I by some action of mine cause you to regret what you have so lovingly done: The I pray that God will let me die insted of live and suffer. Quite a long time ago I had formed it in my imagination how nice it would be and how happy I could be with you my Lydia love. But my power of imagination of that time has proven itself wholly unable to doing justice at forming an outline of happiness. For my darling the present real excites my imaginary one by far, and the prospect for the future are more promising now than they ever have been before, and so let each day pass pleasantly for each that passes; passes only to bring my own Martella and I one day nearer to time that we can claim each other openly to the world. Goodnight dear love it is ten and I will go to rest thinking of you my own.

Ever your Joe

A letter printed from the original from Joe Reuter to Lydia Martella Gillis prior to their marriage.

Sedro, Washington
May 3, 1894

Lydia my Own True Love,
　　Your letter this evening pleased me very much because it showed how thoughtfull you was and how carefull you were of your Joe, for I had intended to go to prayer meeting but as soon as I read your loving and sensible command I made up my mind to at once comply and stay at home to night. I wrote a few lines and thought that Albert had taken it up but now I see that it is still here so I will enclose this also.

Goodnight, darling

E. HAMMER,
dealer in
GENERAL MERCHANDISE
Burlington, Wash. June 18th 1894

Miss Lydia M. Gillis

Sedro Washington

My Own Darling,
Last night I arrived at Mt. Vernon at ten o'clock and I went to bed in a few minutes after that and I am so happy with the knowlege that tomorrow night I can claim you to the world as my own loving Lydia. Oh! how I have been longing for the time to come. Although you dear one made the time pass very pleasently for your Joe. And now my darling we will live for God; and each other. We will close our ears to the world and its talk and that way we will live a happy life and make each other happy. There will be times when we can not have just what we would like to have or what we should have. But if we trust in God he will provide for us what ever is well for us to have. With you my darling at my side I can work with pleasure and even if I do get tired while working I can easy rest up with the darling wife at my side at home. And I am not in the least afraid but what you will be first as much of a home darling as I would like for you to be, and one thing I will promise you now and I want you to remind me of it if I ever should happen to forget it. That is that I will never talk when you are talking and by doing that we will never have any hot words, as some people do, they are not nice to have, and don't do any good.

Well; if your father don't want to take part tomorrow night he can just leave it alone and I will take you dear one myself and save him the trouble for it will be no trouble for me. But a great pleasure insted, I was very glad to receive your letter Saturday and I am very much pleased to know that my darling would not let any man kiss her even tho it were stile, which thank God it is not. I am waiting for Walter and it is time for me to go to the train. With truest love for you my darling I close with a loving kiss which I will deliver with this letter. Ever your Joe.

"Did you ask Uncle Albert to tell you more about Joseph?" I was eager to hear more about this man.

"Heavens, no, I just kept it to myself. I was not much older than Lydia and you don't tell secrets. Joseph was five years older than Lydia and one year older than Albert. Lydia had just turned eighteen and I was nineteen at the time. I was one of Lydia's bridesmaids," said Josephine.

"Tell me more about the wedding," I prodded.

"It was the most beautiful wedding of the season. Lydia's dress was stunning, and they made a very handsome couple. They took the train to Annacortes for their honeymoon and then went to Three Lakes, where Joseph was the new foreman at the shingle mill. Summer was a very busy time and he had to get to work," said Josephine.

"Did you see them after they moved to Three Lakes?"

"Quite a bit, Three Lakes was thirty miles from Sedro Woolley and both towns were busy with people back and forth all the time. Things were booming and McKinley was running for President against William Jennings Bryan. There was a lot of excitement at this time. Henry Ford was talking about his gasoline engine that would take the place of horses someday."

"What did you do for fun when you got together?"

"We had picnics in the park all summer, it was always cooler to be outside as much as possible. Albert and Walter were such show offs. They were in all the Shakespearean plays and wore those ancient costumes, of course we all had to attend every performance," said Josephine.

"We thought we would never see Walter again. After he went to China the whole country erupted. It was called the Boxer Rebellion. Walter, Nellie and Ithiel had to go into hiding or they would have been massacred. They were hidden under the floor of a house for a year. The family endangered their own lives to protect them."

***

The house on Alexander street was sturdy and well built; the covered porch was a pleasant and busy place for the family to spend their leisure time. The grounds were abundant with flowers and blackberry bushes. A small area was fenced for the rabbits that the children kept as pets.

It was rare for the house to ever be silent; there was music all the time. Father played the fiddle and all the children played instruments.

Janette was a firm but gentle woman, who had to keep her husband John in line as best she could, for he was a tease and never took anything seriously. The children loved his antics, and this behavior would lead to a stern reprimand from their mother, whom they adored.

John suffered from bouts of gout and poor circulation, so he spent much of his time in his easy chair with his foot elevated to ease the pain. This position did not interfere with his ability to shout his demands. "Walter? Ernest? Laurence? My God, would somebody listen to me! I am in great pain and nobody cares," yelled John.

"What is all the commotion in here? Are you making that noise all by yourself?" asked Janette.

"Mother, where are your sons? I want some help so I can get out on the porch; its too nice of a day to waste it indoors."

"They are coming. They were helping Albert clear his drive. The bushes were taking over the road, and it was near impossible to get to the house," said Janette.

"I told Albert a while back to get those bushes trimmed and he didn't listen to me," said John.

"What is the matter, Momma?" said Lydia as she and Rosalie came in from picking berries.

"Poppa is having another attack of gout, and he can't get himself out to the porch. Make him some tea till the boys can help him." said Janette.

"Momma, Laurence climbed up on the roof of Albert's house and wouldn't come down to help us clear the road. I am full of stickers and Walter rode his bicycle to the school; he said he had to practice for a play," said Ernest.

"Poppa needs your help right now. You can tell him all about it once you get him settled on the porch," said Janette.

Ernest went to help his father who was lying on the floor with his feet in the air.

"It's about time you got here, I was going to roll out the door and get the ax to chop off my foot. It's throbbing like a balloon about to burst."

Ernest was really upset that he had to help his father all by himself. He swore under his breath at his brothers who had deserted him.

"Here, Poppa, let me help you get to the porch," It was quite a struggle getting him into a standing position so he could hobble to the porch. Both were in a sweat and out of breath when they finished the task.

"Here's some tea, Poppa," said Rosalie as she came through the door. "Ernest, Momma has some food for you in the kitchen, if you are hungry."

"I'm going to be picking stickers out of me till kingdom comes," said Ernest as he headed for the kitchen.

Janette thanked her lucky stars every day, that out of her six children she had these two daughters to help keep some order to the household. The four boys were every bit as mischievous as their father.

The women were very busy at this time making dresses and fancy shirts; they liked to keep up with the fashions. They prided themselves on their seventeen inch waists. Even so, they wore their corsets daily. Janette carried herself very straight, never stoop shouldered and she stressed this to all her children.

Walter came up the path on his bicycle and announced that he had to have a costume for the play.

"You have a week to make my costume. I'll show you what it looks like," said Walter as he ruffled through his bag of papers.

"A week? We can't make that costume in a week, we would have to sew into the night with all the lanterns burning." said Lydia.

"When is the play?" asked Janette.

"Well, it's not for three weeks, but we have to have rehearsals," said Walter.

"You don't have to wear your costume for rehearsals," said Lydia. "That will give us more time, and we won't have to sew at night."

"Did you leave Laurence on the roof at Albert's?" asked Janette. "We haven't seen him all afternoon."

"I'll go over to Albert's and see if he is still there," said Walter as he hopped on his bicycle.

Albert was the oldest son, tall and handsome with thick wavy hair and dark eyes. He had married his childhood sweetheart. They lived within walking distance.

Walter was just as handsome as Albert, only he wore a full handle bar mustache and was very much in demand for the school plays. He loved to act and wear the costumes with such flair. Acting to him was very enjoyable, but he was destined to be a missionary. The thought of traveling all over the world to help people of other cultures was fascinating to him. He was planning to leave for his first assignment as soon as he finished his schooling.

Walter and Albert went together to start the SKAGIT COUNTY TIMES. They were both printers by trade and when they weren't acting in the local plays they found other jobs that put them in touch with interesting news items. The TIMES was doing so well they decided to expand and start a paper in Issaquah. This kept them hopping, but Walter never lost sight of his true calling as a missionary.

Lydia was the oldest of the girls, slender and demure. She was meticulous in her dress and a very fine seamstress.

"Rosalie, measure my waist for me, my new skirt has to fit perfectly," said Lydia.

"When are you going to find time to sew on your skirt? You have to make Walter's costume first," said Rosalie as she measured Lydia around her waist. "You are sixteen and a half, you must have lost some weight or you are lacing your corset too tight."

"I am not, it's normal to change size when you reach seventeen," replied Lydia. "I'm going to make my new dress with the leg-o-mutton sleeves; they're the latest fashion."

"Now that I am thirteen, I can have a dress like that too, can't I?" asked Rosalie.

"Oh, no, I saw a really nice dress that you should have. I'll help you make it as soon as we finish the costume." said Lydia.

Ernest was just two years younger than Lydia. He liked to build things and was always making a mess for the girls to clean up. Janette tried to get him to fix the chairs that always needed repair. He would rather torment the girls.

The boys always had to balance themselves on two legs, they never sat in a chair properly.

" I was only trying to rescue Aunt Myrtle's cat. He was frightened and couldn't get down by himself. I can't help it if the cat wouldn't come to me. I had to coax him to trust me," said Laurence.

"You only went up on the roof to get out of work. The cat came down a long time ago," said Walter walking out to the porch to visit with his father.

"Ah, Walter, be a good chap and fetch me my pipe," said John.

Walter enjoyed sitting on the porch with his father and especially liked the aroma of the pipe.

"Hello, David, how was the fishing?" John hollered at his brother-in-law as he was walking up the path from the river.

"I got a nice mess for a couple meals. They were biting real good early this morning. They weren't too hungry this afternoon, so I called it quits," said David.

"As soon as I get this darn fool foot calmed down, I'm gonna show you the best fishin' hole in the State of Washington. Not many know about this spot, but I'll show you 'cause I can't get down there by myself anymore, and I'm gonna need your help. Pull up that chair and set a spell," said John.

"Hey, Walter, it won't be long now 'till you will be leavin' the coop," said David as he put down his fishing pole and sat down facing the horizon in all its glory.

"Yes, Sir, I still have three more months of schooling," said Walter.

Meanwhile, Laurence was in the kitchen trying to convince his mother that he really wanted to save the cat. He was the youngest of the children and needed his mother's attention more than the rest. He was handsome in a different way than his brothers, but still tall and slender.

"Laurence, set that chair up right. We won't have a single chair to sit on if you keep that up," scolded Janette. "We are ready to sit down to supper. Go tell your father and ask Uncle David if he wants to eat with us."

Laurence went out the kitchen door and ran around the house to the front porch and flung himself over the railing. "Momma says supper is ready and you can eat with us too, Uncle David."

"Well, I don't want to be any bother, but I would be obliged to accept," David said the same thing every time he was invited to share a meal with his sister's family.

Laurence did a back flip over the railing and ran smack into a tree that he knew was there. He landed flat on his back and knocked the wind out of him.

"Mrs. Gillis, you better come take care of your rapscallion, he's done it again," said John.

Janette rushed over to her gasping son and gave him caresses to get his wind back. "Laurence you won't live to see twelve if you keep this up." She helped him to the kitchen and supper was uneventful after that.

David was a bachelor and did odd jobs. He never wanted to be tied down to a steady job or a wife. He would find a room with a family and that way he never had to have any responsibility. A boarding house fixed his meals and did his laundry.

"As it turns out, I'm going to have to find another boarding house. Mrs. Burtel thinks I should be married and she won't let up. She asked me what I thought of Maude Lundgren and I told her I wouldn't marry her if she was the last woman on earth. I can't stay there any longer," said David.

The room was very quiet and Janette looked at Lydia and Lydia looked at Rosalie, words were not necessary with the look. They were waiting for Poppa to invite David to live with them and hoping he wouldn't. This would mean more laundry and cleaning and waiting on him for her and the girls. As if they needed any more chores.

Then the silence was shattered. "David you should live here with us. We have room. By golly, we can go fishing every day. Isn't that right, Mrs. Gillis?" said John.

He always called his wife "Mrs. Gillis" when he wanted to make a point that his decision was final.

Janette had to leave the table hastily before she said too much. Why was she so resentful? He is her brother and she should be happy to have him live with them. She struggled with herself before she returned to the table.

"Of course, you should live with us, David. John is right," conceded Janette.

The men retired to the parlor as the women cleaned up after the meal.

"Momma, how are we going to get all the sewing done and take care of Uncle David's needs too," said Lydia.

"Not only does Walter need a costume, but we have to make him a suit before he leaves on assignment," added Rosalie.

"I know this will put a lot of extra work on both of you, but we will have to do the best we can. He can have the east room upstairs. Walter can share his room with Ernest till he leaves," consoled Janette.

John's foot eased, up and he was able to go fishing with David with the aid of a cart that Ernest and David built so John wouldn't have to walk. It was easy to pull, but they had to rig up a brake or John would have gone sailing right into the river.

***

It wasn't long before the extra work took its toll. Rosalie was complaining of back pains and extreme tiredness.

"Lydia go fetch the Doctor." said Janette.

"I'll hurry, Momma, I hope Rosalie will be all right," said Lydia.

It was just a short distance to town, but that day it seemed like it took forever.

After examining Rosalie the Doctor said, "I can't treat her for this at home, she is going to have to go into the hospital for tests. Sedro Woolley doesn't have the facilities for what I think is Rosalie's ailment. She will have to go to Anacortes as soon as possible. It may be kidney failure."

"Momma, I can go with her to the hospital," said Lydia.

"No, you need to stay here and take care of your Poppa and the house and cook the meals," said Janette. "I'll bring my buggy over and we will make her comfortable. I have to go with her to the hospital anyway," said the doctor. "If we leave right now, we can be there by dark."

Lydia was very concerned about her sister and wanted to be with her at this time, but she knew her mother depended on her to stay. This is where she needed to be.

Annacortes, thirty miles away on Puget Sound, was the closest hospital for major operations.

The next day Janette came home with the doctor. She was exhausted and needed to rest before she returned to the hospital.

"Have they learned from the tests yet, Momma? Will they have to operate?" asked Lydia. "Rosalie is in a lot of pain, but she was able to sleep some last night. The doctor said they can't wait too long to operate. I am going to get some rest and return with the doctor this afternoon. I will sit up with her all night and they will operate first thing in the morning," said Janette.

"Doctor Brooks is the best around and he knows what he is doing. Rosalie will come out of this in good shape. Don't worry about us, we can take care of things here," said John.

Janette returned to the hospital to wait until morning and wait again while they operated.

Finally the doctor emerged from the operating room and told

Janette, "The operation went well, we had to remove one kidney. It had stopped working completely and was a strain on her good one. We got it in time before it weakened her good one. She will have to stay here for at least two weeks, barring any complications. You can go see her as soon as she wakes and then you go home and get some rest," said the doctor.

"Momma, I brought the buggy to take you home. How is Rosalie? Is the operation over?" asked Walter

Oh, Walter, they removed one kidney. We can see her when she wakes," said Janette.

"Mrs.Gillis, you can see your daughter now, she is asking for you," said the nurse.

Janette made many trips to the hospital during the next two weeks. Sometimes with Walter and sometimes with the doctor.

Lydia did her best to run the house, but she was tiring and was anxious for Rosalie to come home.

The whole family was so happy to see Rosalie when she was finally released from the hospital. She was very weak and it would take weeks for her to recuperate from her surgery, but at least she was home and Lydia would take care of her.

Rosalie could do some of the hand stitching while she was resting and Lydia had the sewing machine going most of the day. Walter's costume was finished and his suit would be ready in time for his assignment.

"Momma, I am going to town to get some lace for my dress and buttons for Rosalie's dress," said Lydia. "Walter can give you a ride on his bicycle," said Janette.

"I don't mind walking. It has been so long since we have walked to town; I miss getting out," said Lydia.

Lydia walked briskly and enjoyed the sun. The path was dry most of the way. They had rain just a couple days ago and everything was so fresh. The closer she got to town the muddier it was. She had to hike her skirts and step around the puddles.

"Oh, why didn't I ask Walter to give me a ride on his bicycle? I'll be all muddy when I get home," she said to herself.

The town of Sedro Woolley was small and everyone knew everyone else. As she entered the store the clerk came over to Lydia and asked about Rosalie and her mother.

"It is so good to have them home and they are both doing well, catching up on their rest," answered Lydia. "Are you going to the dance on Saturday? There is a potluck supper before the dance," said the clerk.

"Yes, I wouldn't miss that for the world. Rosalie said she felt strong enough to go and sit on the side. She doesn't want to miss it. I need some lace and buttons to finish our dresses. We have been so busy trying to get all the sewing done," said Lydia.

"Isn't the school play on Sunday night?" asked the clerk.

"Yes, Walter has rehearsal, every night this week, I think he is ready," said Lydia

***

John was dressed and ready to go to the potluck supper. His gout was under control, so he was feeling pretty good.

Janette and Lydia had spent the morning preparing the food for the potluck and now were trying to get dressed and help Rosalie as well.

"Laurence, if you aren't ready in five minutes, we are leaving without you. Ernest, get the buggy and put in the food. Where is Walter?" demanded John.

"Walter is already there. He and David are helping to set up tables and chairs. We are ready, let's go," said Janette.

John let Ernest drive the buggy and they were on their way. "You take care of the horses and make sure they get water, Ernest. Laurence you help clean up after the supper.

Walter will show you which tables to leave. Don't climb up in the trees to get out of work."

"John, it's good to see you up and about. How's your foot? Mrs. Gillis, good day to you. I hear you have been busy taking care of the sick," said Mr. Donough, the mayor of Sedro Woolley.

"Thank you, and we are doing well, Rosalie is getting stronger every day," replied John.

Janette made it a point to sit by her friends so she could catch up on all the news, Lydia helped Rosalie find a place by her friends, and her friends were close by also.

Most of the families had several children and they all attended the same school from first grade to graduation. The teachers lived with some of the families. It was always fun to attend the school functions whether it was a dance or the school play, the whole town turned out.

This was printed in the "Skagit County Times" owned by Walter and Albert Gillis in 1898

Lydia wrote this on Feb. 22, 1898 when our Grandma Mary Kerr died in Petrolia, Ont. Canada, where I was born on Feb. 22, 1882

Aunt Rosalie (Hayden)

Dearest Grandma, God hath called thee,
From thy earthly home below,
To a brighter, fairer country,
Better far than this we know.

Friends and kindred sadly miss thee,
Weep and mourn for thee in vain,
But we have the blest assurance,
That our loss is thy great gain.
God knew best, though we may wonder,
Why the death-damp chilled thy brow,
Christ said: Ye shall know hereafter,
What I do; ye know not now.

Yes, dear Grandma we will meet thee
In that better world above,
Where there is no pain nor sorrow,
But where all is peace and love.

Lydia Reuter

CHAPTER 2

THREE LAKES, WASHINGTON 1900

It is now 1900 and immigrants are flocking to the United States. The economy is booming and Henry Ford is the talk of the town.

Walter had been spending a lot of time in Issaquah getting the paper started. While he was there, he met the woman he would marry, Helen Chadwick, of Hood's Canal.

They planned a wedding for August 19 in Seattle at the Diller Hotel. Helen's brother, George Chadwick, was Walter's attendant and Rosalie Gillis was the bride's maid.

Lydia and Joseph had their fourth child by this time and since baby John was just a few months old, they didn't attend her brother's wedding.

Rosalie spent a lot of time with Lydia, sewing and watching the children. Lydia was a practical nurse and would leave on the spur of a moment to help with a birthing or to care for someone who was ill.

In February Albert and Josephine had their first baby, he was named Guy Alfred, but on June 5th he died of unknown causes. By September Josephine was expecting another child.

Albert was kept busy working the two papers when in March of 1902 he got blood poisoning and died. He was only thirty. Two months later Josephine gave birth to twins, Horatio and Beatrice. It was a very sad time for all the family.

Lydia and Joseph had four children Janet, Rose, Charles, and John. They all arrived from Three Lakes for Albert's funeral.

They all congregated at the house which was bustling with

everyone grieving and trying to console Josephine and Janette. John was in so much misery from his gout and rheumatism, he tried to find a place to ease his pain in his own way.

Aunt Rosalie had just finished her training as a practical nurse and was trying to be as helpful and comforting as she could be to anyone who needed consoling. She was a very attractive woman and had lots of suitors, but she was not ready to marry and settle down just yet. She was urged to find a husband, soon, or she would end up an Old Maid.

Walter and Nellie were on their way to Mexico, his first assignment as a missionary. They delayed their trip to attend Albert's funeral.

Ernest and Laurence were eighteen and sixteen now and still as mischievous as ever.

Janette was so glad that Aunt Rosalie was still at home to help her.

One year later, just a month after Lydia gave birth to her fifth child, Joseph James. Mr. Gillis's health failed drastically, and he died, partly from his ailment and partly from his grief of Albert's death. Services were held at the Presbyterian Church, which he built in his prime, as a Contractor. All of the town knew him. Janette was comforted by the consoling friends, but all the troubles arriving at once threw Janette into ill health herself, and Aunt Rosalie devoted as much time as she could to her mother. They struggled from day to day just to keep the family together.

Then word came that Joseph's father had died in Ohio and his mother was alone. Joseph couldn't go to Ohio at this time, so he sent word to his mother to get her affairs in order and as soon as possible to take the train to Washington to stay with them.

This would be a hardship on the family, as Joseph's family wasn't wealthy and they didn't have the money to go to his father's funeral and the cost of moving his mother would put a strain on their pocketbook.

The children had never met Joseph's parents, so, having Grandma Reuter come to live with them was going to be different.

They wondered if she was as nice as Grandma Janette. She wouldn't be coming right away, as it takes time to settle affairs.

Meanwhile, the children enjoyed going to Puget Sound to play on the logs in the river. Lydia was busy with the new baby and Janet kept an eye on John, who was only three. Things were getting back to normal after Grandpa John's and Albert's funerals were over. Rose was just starting first grade and Janet was in third. Rose wasn't very happy about leaving her momma and going to school, but she and Janet walked to school together with all the other kids from the neighborhood.

Janet and Rose had a plan to get out of school. They decided if Rose would start crying then the teacher would have to get Janet out of class to take Rose home. This worked three or four times before their momma got wise. Each time they had to walk next to the railroad tracks by themselves to get home. So their momma arranged to have some of the railroad workers scare them the next time it happened. The railroad workers waited for them to show up, and they jumped out of the bushes and chased them almost all the way home. Needless to say they didn't pull that trick any more.

The children were busy with school and Lydia was very busy taking care of Charles, John and Joe. Lydia liked the times everyone could all go to Sedro Woolley and visit Grandma Janette. Charles and John were getting bigger now and not so much trouble. The children could hardly wait to get to Grandmas'. She wasn't very far from the Skagit River and Poppa had told them he didn't want the children on the logs.

It was so much fun to ride the logs, the children couldn't resist and the four of them were riding down the logs when Poppa showed up. He was very angry with them for disobeying him. He grabbed the log the children were on and gave it a hard tug spilling them into the river. The children hung on to each other around the waist and thought they were going to drown, when Poppa pulled them out.

He said, "Now, I told you how dangerous it was to play on the logs, have you learned your lesson?"

"Yes, Poppa, we are sorry, we won't do it again," they all said shivering.

When they got back to grandmas', their momma was fit to be tied. She was such a fragile woman and having five children so soon wore her down. "You will be the death of me yet," she said, drying them off and hugging each one at the same time. "I could have lost all of you, and then what would I do?"

Grandma Reuter had to get several affidavits to prove that she was married to Grandpa, before she could get the widows' pension. Grandpa was in the Civil War and he had been getting his military pension when he got sick with chronic rheumatism, later he had to have his leg amputated.

Just before he died he went insane and Grandma had to take care of him for several months.

After she got her widow's pension, of twelve dollars a month, she made arrangements for her trip to Washington. She wanted to go to Canada where her daughter lived, but she had so many children, she wasn't sure they had room for her.

Joseph was making more money now at the shingle mill, so they sent him to Sperling, closer to Sedro Woolley. Lydia was elated at the news. She could see more of her family and the children could walk to their Grandmas' house. Her brothers would give them rides on their bicycles.

She missed spending time with her sister and mother.

Now she could help with some of the sewing.

Grandma Reuter was having trouble adjusting to her new home and the rowdiness of the children. She would sit and crochet most of the day.

Just about the time baby Joe was able to walk and feed himself Momma discovered she was going to have another baby. No wonder she had been feeling so tired.

The children were disappointed in their Grandma Reuter. Instead of getting to know them she scolded them. They stayed outside most of the time or at their other Grandma's house.

Lydia had her hands full, although Janet was a lot of help to her, especially when it came time for the birth of the baby. Several hours later a baby girl was born. Lydia was exhausted and needed several days to get her strength back. Janet did most of the cooking and Aunt Rosalie gave her a hand with the children. The rest of the children tried to be as good as they could be and not upset their Momma.

Janet and Rosa said they wanted to name their new baby sister. They named her Ruth Naomi.

Grandma Reuter would cook a meal now and then, but the children didn't like what she cooked, and she got very angry with the children. Joseph tried to console her, but she wasn't happy with them.

As time went on the children spent a lot of time at Grandma Gillis'. They liked to play with the rabbits and they would carry the cat to visit also. The children loved to pick the ripe berries for Grandma. They would eat most of them, but whatever was left, she turned into pies and jelly.

When Walter postponed his trip to Mexico, another minister was sent in his place. In the mean time he was sent to Oakland, California, to serve the needy. He was informed that there was a place for him now. So he and his wife Nellie and their six year old son, Ithiel, prepared to leave for Mexico.

Lydia was having trouble breathing and taking care of the children was becoming more difficult each day. She needed more help than Grandma Reuter could give, and Janet was doing more and more of the housework. Joseph was concerned over his wife's health and suggested that his mother should go stay with his sister in Canada. He would make arrangements with his sister as soon as possible.

Joseph put his mother on the train to Sault Ste Marie, Ontario, Canada, a month later.

Joseph's job took him back to Three Lakes. Moving his sick wife and six children was not an easy task. The Company furnished him a house, and all he had to do was move in.

A postcard from Lydia to her mother Janette Gillis: The front is a picture of the school at Three Lakes with all the students posed in front of the school. 1908

Dear Mamma,
I am so glad you are improving. Don't forget to keep my roses till I send for them. You want to pack them good so they won't get crushed. Sometime next week I will let you know. My throat is sore today can hardly speak. I take a cold as fast as I start to get better. How is all the rest? E.S. is well, I hope.
(E.S.?) Lovingly,
Lydia

The doctor made regular visits to the house to check on Lydia. He said she had tuberculosis; she needed to be isolated and bed rest.

Joseph hired a woman to take care of the children and attend to his wife, but she was afraid she would get the disease.

Lydia wanted to go to her mother so her sister Rosalie could take care of her. "Please, take me back to Sedro Woolley, Joseph, you can bring the children later," said Lydia

Lydia returned to Sedro Woolley and Grandma sent for Aunt Rosalie to come home and take care of her sister.

Aunt Rosalie was beside herself when she heard about Lydia. She knew her mother couldn't take care of Lydia, because she wasn't all that well herself.

Aunt Rosalie packed up her belongings and left for Sedro Woolley.

Joseph decided the children should start school in Sedro Woolley. It would be easier for Aunt Rosalie to get them off to school than for him. Janet was old enough to help with the younger children, too.

Christmas was not a happy time for the family. Lydia took a turn for the worse right after the first of the year. Grandma sent Rose to town to fetch the doctor. "Hurry, now, don't dawdle, your momma is very sick and she needs the doctor right away".

Rose took off down the street yelling "My momma is dying, my momma is dying." When she got to the doctors' house there were tears streaming down her face; she couldn't talk. She just pointed to her Grandmas' house. The doctor grabbed his bag and followed her home.

CHAPTER 3

1909

Orphaned
Sault Ste Marie, Ontario, Canada
Kit Carson, Colorado

Lydia died the end of January. Joseph knew his time was running out, the pain in his gut was excruciating. The doctor urged him to go to the hospital, but he refused. There were arrangements to be made with his sister to take the children. Ida Bea and her husband Joshua Clem, agreed to take the children, in spite of the hardship it would confer on their family, even with the money Joseph was sending for their care.

Their Grandma Gillis, who lived in Sedro Woolley had no children living at home, Uncle Walter was thirty five and had come home for his sister's funeral, he would return to China for his new assignment in a few days, as a missionary. Uncle Ernest was twenty nine and a carpenter, his home was nearby. Aunt Rosalie was twenty seven and lived with her mother, Janette

Then there was Laurence, he married Myrtle and moved in with Grandma.

Grandma Gillis had a brother, David, who lived in a room upstairs and since John's death never came down to join the rest of the family, he would go fishing and bring back his catch and cook them for himself.

Joseph appointed a lawyer to handle the children's inheritance. Joshua Clem was to receive so much a month for the children's care.

Lydias' family was very upset when they found out about Josephs' plan, but he told them he was a sick man and he would not live another year. He wanted the children to be with his family. Joseph didn't get along with Lydia's family.

The children stayed in Sedro Woolley, with Grandma Gillis, while Joseph took care of all the arrangements for Lydia's burial.

Friends and family tried to console the children as best they could, but the children knew their time was short to remain here in the place they called the only home they ever knew. They wanted to stay with the people they loved.

Joseph had finished all his business in Sedro Woolley, and it was time to return to Three Lakes.

The children climbed into the horse-drawn cart for the thirty mile journey to Three Lakes. They spent the summer months with Joseph until his health started to fail. They knew it was just a matter of time before he would be gone, also.

In September Joseph went to the hospital in Snohomish. The children were put on a train and sent to Joshua Clem's in Sault Ste Marie, Ontario, Canada. Their Aunt Rosalie fixed a basket of fried chicken for them to take on their journey.

General Hospital
Snohomish, Wa.
Sept. 24-1909

Dear Daughter Rosa,
Soon you will be in a new home and I hope it will be an honest home no matter how poor the people may be you will have a chance to grow up to be a true woman. And as you like to play quite well I hope you will have a horse to ride and you can also train calves so that you can ride them. And I want you to make yourself understand that you are big and old enough to make your living and schooling for yourself if you will only make yourself agreeable to the people you are with and that will leave the use of that money for the help of Dear Ruth and Joseph is small yet, but before long he will be able to make his own way in the right kind of home. And I want you to love Anna very much for

no girl ever had a better sister than she is, and she loves you very dearly. Still I told her first what I am going to tell you. And that is this, please get yourselves into different homes for there's not anybody that need two girls so near the same size.

With my prayers for your welfare, Good by
Your Papa

(Reprinted from Joseph James Reuter's original handwritten letter to his daughter Rosa, from his hospital bed.)

The children began their adventure on the train from the State of Washington to Canada. Janet, the eldest daughter was in charge of her younger brothers and sisters. Janet was fourteen, Rosalie was twelve, Charles was ten, John was nine, Joseph was six and baby Ruth was four.

It was not an easy journey. There was a train wreck in Montana and part of the rain turned over. The children were so frightened they stayed in their seats and waited for the train crew to get the train working again. The part of the train they were in did not turn over, to the relief of all the children. The wreck delayed their arrival in Canada and there was no way to let Aunt Ida Bea know what had happened. Charles was not well; he was the sickly one. He took his parents deaths very hard, but didn't show it. He suffered in silence. He never complained and was no trouble at all. Janet watched over him and tried to comfort him as best she could. She was like a mother to little Ruth, also.

Rosalie and Janet relied on each other to keep up their spirits and keep their brothers occupied during the long journey to Canada. It was easy to keep an eye on all of them, as none of them wanted to get very far away from each other. None the less, Janet had her hands full.

The journey took them through the badlands of Montana and South Dakota, which were only territories at this time. Miles of desolate country with no sign of a tree.

They had to change trains in Fargo and continue on the Soo Line to Duluth and cross the Great Lakes. Finally they arrived in

Canada. Poppa died early in October, shortly after they arrived. It was as though he waited until they had safely arrived at their destination.

Now Aunt Ida Bea and Joshua had eleven children of their own and seven children still living at home when her brother's children arrived. Effie was seventeen, Lora Imo thirteen, Frantz eleven, Wendell nine, Rose seven, Nancy Jane three and Earl one year old.

Their eldest daughter, Hyma was married and had one child already, she lived next door.

After their arrival the children were kept busy harvesting the vegetables and getting them ready for storage through the winter. They were enrolled in school with their cousins.

Christmas and the New Year came and went. They trudged through the snow to school and went through the motions of living from day to day. In spite of the drudgery, there were some happy times when they skated on the river and watched the northern lights dance across the sky.

Joshua Clem had the ability to make cups dance on the shelves, without even touching them. This made the children a little wary about their uncle and none wanted to displease him.

Joseph's plan had been for the children to live in Canada, but little did he know that Joshua Clem had other plans for the children. He heard about homesteaders in Colorado who had to relinquish their land because of hardships or deaths. So he contacted the department that handled relinquishments and staked his claim. He had so many days to show up and claim the land, so he took off for Colorado.

Finally it was May, it had been a long and lonely winter even with thirteen children in one house. One morning they were awakened to the most awful wailing and commotion that they had ever heard. "What's happening?" cried all the children at the same time.

"People are running through the streets yelling that the world is coming to an end," said Aunt Ida Bea. "A huge comet was spotted and the tail was so long you could see it for miles. They are calling it Haley's Comet. The people are running in circles, they don't know where to go; they are just frightened and screaming."

One neighbor hanged himself. They found him hanging in the barn. All the neighbors are gathered in the street in front of their houses, afraid to be alone.

Aunt Ida Bea was trying to comfort and calm the children; she was hysterical herself. She was just rambling on about all the bad things that were happening.

Rose and her brothers and sisters were so frightened; so much had happened to them and now this. Rose started crying, "I want to go home to my Momma, I want my Momma, I don't like it here." The other children noticed that Rose had a red streak that ran down the middle of her forehead to the tip of her nose, it always showed up when she was upset.

It took several days for the crisis to be over, and people started realizing that they hadn't perished. But the fanatics were still around urging everyone to repent and be saved and join the church.

Soon after the crisis of the comet calmed down, Aunt Ida Bea got word from Joshua that he got his land and that they were to pack up and come to Kit Carson, Colorado.

Aunt Ida Bea didn't have the money for everyone to go at this time, so she contacted the lawyer and told him the Reuter children needed funds to send them to Kit Carson. She then sent her brother's children ahead by themselves.

Joshua Clem also knew that this move to the States would put him in control of the orphans' money. He wouldn't have to account to the lawyer for every penny he spent.

The train went through Chicago and Kansas City. When the train stopped at the station, there was a crowd of people waiting to see the orphans. They continued on their journey to Joplin, Missouri. There they were greeted the same way. It was early July and fire-crackers were going off everywhere.

Each stop that the train made was greeted by the townspeople who wanted to see the orphans. The news had traveled ahead, that there were six orphans traveling alone. This was not unheard of in this day and age, as many orphan trains were transporting orphans from eastern cities. But it was rare to see six from the same family and there were so many dangers that could befall them. It was not a good idea to have this many children traveling so far a distance without someone to watch over them.

Uncle Joshua met them at the train when it arrived in Kit Carson. All the people were in town for the Fourth of July celebration, and the children arriving at the same time just added to the excitement of the day. It was July 4, 1910.

Uncle Joshua was impatient and wanted them to hurry up and get on his wagon; he was in a hurry to get going. It was very hot, and the wagon didn't have any sides on it. They had to hang on to keep from falling off on the rough ride to their new home.

When they arrived at their new place, the children looked around and all they saw was a tent. "Where's the house?" someone said.

"That's where you will live until I get good and ready to start the dugout. Now put your bags in the tent and get some supper started," said Uncle Joshua.

Uncle Joshua had squandered and drank up all of the wealth he had been given to care for the children. So it was going to be a struggle to survive out here on the prairie. Aunt Ida Bea and her children, along with Grandma Reuter, arrived a couple of months later. Surprisingly, the eldest daughter and her husband and two year old daughter decided to come with the rest of the family; she was also expecting another child.

Now, there were nineteen people in this God forsaken place, living in a tent!! That is the entire population of some small towns. It's hard to believe that so many people went along with this maniac's plan. He had to be the con man of the century.

Aunt Ida Bea was a screaming banshee, and she insisted that Joshua get busy and finish the dugout so they could have a better place to live in before the weather changed. She couldn't believe that she had left her modest house and gardens for this.

Joshua Clem didn't pay much attention to his hysterical wife, but he did proceed to attack the dugout because the homestead act also pertained to relinquishments. Improvements must be made to the land during the first year or they would lose the land.

Clem was busy mixing concrete for the walls of the dugout. The boys were recruited to help haul the mixture and pour the walls. Then he formed the ceiling and covered it with sod.

Inside the tent was sweltering, and so the children spent a lot of time outside in the shade, when they weren't doing chores. It was the only place they could find that gave them some shelter from the heat. They were kept busy hauling water and fire wood. Washing clothes and cooking meals was not an easy ordeal.

When the rains came, which wasn't very often, the Big Sandy river would fill up with a gully washer. When the Big Sandy was full, teams of horses had to pull wagons across the river, sometimes they would lose the whole outfit in the quick sand. The only way the children could get to town was over the Big Sandy. They would carry their clothes on their heads to cross, and hope that they made it before the quick sand got them.

It was a treat; they could see their classmates. This was the only way they had of getting away from their drunken uncle. They didn't dare let on that they were being mistreated. They were frightened of his wrath.

They went to the stores in town. There were two of them, one on each side of the railroad tracks. Rhoades was on one side and Waggoners was on the other. Next to the tracks was a saloon owned by Rattlesnake Pete. He got his name because he killed so many rattlesnakes.

After the children started school, it became evident that Uncle Joshua was trying to get Rose alone. When they went to bed at night Janet would always lay her hand on Rose; that way she would always know if Clem would try to get to Rose during the night.

One of their neighbors noticed that the children were scantily clad in the dead of winter. Janet was pumping water one day when the Meiers' came to visit; her clothes were not suitable for the freezing weather.

Not long after this episode Janet made a plan with the Meier's that on her way to church she would take off in the direction of their ranch and they were waiting for her as planned.

They notified the Judge in Cheyenne Wells of the children's plight and the authorities took the children away from Joshua Clem.

The good citizens of Kit Carson were enraged and drove him out of town and told him to never show his face around there again. He had been seen with a woman in town and rumor has it that they left town together.

Aunt Ida Bea was relieved that he was gone, but she had no way to take care of all the children and her mother.

Janet and Rose were farmed out to work for some of the families in town as maids.

***

1911 began and soon everything would be turned upside down again. Grandma Reuter died. Hyma, the eldest daughter of Ida Bea, lost her baby soon after birth; this brought about the decision for her and her family to return to Sault Ste Marie, Ontario, Canada.

Winter arrived with a fury, it turned out to be the worst blizzard in years, and the decision to send the Reuter children to the orphanage in Denver was made in December 1911.

Janet was sixteen and so she didn't have to go to the orphanage. She could continue working for the Paul Meier family. It was decided that she should move to Cheyenne Wells to live with the McGinty family and attend school there while helping around the house. Rose was fourteen and she could stay with Aunt Ida Bea to help her with the younger children.

Charles, John, Joseph and Ruth began their journey to Denver to enter the State Home for Dependent and Neglected Children on December 16, 1911.

What a way to spend Christmas. This is the third Christmas

without their parents. These are not happy times and Christmas had no meaning for these children.

Rose was all alone now, with her Aunt and cousins. After a month away from her brothers and sisters, she couldn't stand it any longer, so after the first of the year she pleaded with her Aunt to let her go to the orphanage. The authorities were notified. January 12, 1912, Rose arrived at the orphanage.

Aunt Ida Bea continued to live in the dugout, along with her children.

A dugout is not very large, it has a dirt floor, a sod roof and this one had concrete walls. The windows were covered with oil cloth to keep the snow, wind and rain out. Spiders and centipedes love to occupy the corners and drop on you from the ceiling. You always checked your shoes before you put them on.

At The Home for Neglected and Dependent Children, the boys shared a room and Ruth was in the nursery, when Rose arrived she had a room in the girls section. They didn't get to see each other very often, but they tried to see each other between chores.

"Why did they have to take us away from Janet?" asked John.

Rose was now the eldest, and she felt in charge of taking care of her brothers and sister. "I don't know why they sent us here, John, but we have to keep in touch, no matter where they send us. At least here we have a warm bed to sleep in and food," replied Rose.

Days passed and they were assigned chores in the daily routine of running the orphanage. Shortly after they arrived, Rose took sick. They said she had diphtheria, she had to be isolated in the infirmary. She was so sick she thought she was going to die. One day she was so still the nurses thought she had died, so they moved her bed into the hallway with those who were to be removed. But one of the nurses later saw her leg move and they put her back into her hospital room. She survived this illness.

When she got well, she was assigned to the kitchen and the nursery. She was glad that she could see Ruth once in awhile. The boys had to scrub floors and help in the garden, even Charles. Sometimes when he would wet the bed, he had to scrub floors for punishment. His kidneys were bad, and he couldn't control his bladder. This condition would cause him to run a fever. When she could, Rose would try to console him. He was in pain all the time, and the hard work was causing his health to fail.

Rose was fifteen years old now and could be farmed out to families, in town, for domestic help.

She would live with the family as a maid or housekeeper. The first family she was assigned to was named Frasier. They didn't treat her too well and she had to wear clothes that was furnished by the orphanage. The Frasiers didn't want Rose going to the same school as their daughter, and so Rose rode the streetcar to South High School.

John was very angry at the way Charles was treated, and so he and Charles planned a way to leave the orphanage and try to make it on their own. Joe wanted to go with them. Charles said he was too young; they were going to have enough trouble just taking care of themselves.

By this time John and Charles were twelve and thirteen. One night they slipped out of their rooms and made it out of the orphanage. Down the road they went as fast as their legs would carry them. Their freedom was short lived, however, and they were caught the next day and returned to the orphanage. They were punished severely and had to do extra work as part of their punishment. John always believed that Charles was abused by Clem before they went to the orphanage and that caused the kidney damage, the hard work just aggravated it. However, this did not deter them from trying again. The authorities found them and brought them back again. These episodes did not help Charles, and his condition worsened. It was May, 1913. Charles' kidneys failed and he died.

Janet wasn't able to come for his funeral. Word was sent to Rose at the Frasiers and John, Joe and Ruth were helpless to do anything. Charles was buried in paupers field at Riverside Cemetery in Denver.

After the funeral Janet wrote to Rose and urged her to promise to keep in touch with each other as often as they could. John could always find Janet in Kit Carson. Joe was taken in by a family from Kansas, but not adopted.

Rose was not happy with the Frasiers, and they were not happy with her either. Back to the orphanage she went to wait for another family to need her services.

Rose then was sent to another family to work. The Palmers. Mr. Palmer was a Judge and they entertained a lot, and Mother Palmer needed someone to help her when she put on these socials.

Life at the Palmer's was so much better than at the Frasier's for Rosalie. She so hoped that life would start to get better for her now.

She wrote to Janet and let her know where she was. She felt very much alone now. It was November and John had been sent to Pueblo to work in the coal mines.

A family wanted to adopt Ruth, and she would be leaving in December. That left Joe at the orphanage by himself. It would be so good if some one would adopt him, also.

When Rose walked to the streetcar on her way to school she would pass the school yard where Ruth was on the playground. She would stop and visit with her. One day the older sister of Ruth's new family told Rose that Ruth belonged to them now and she was not to see her again. Very soon after that Ruth's new family moved to Illinois.

Rose concentrated on her chores and house cleaning. Doing the laundry was a real chore. By the time you set up the tubs and heated the water, sorted the clothes, it was an all day job. It seemed everyone did their laundry on the same day every week, it was a routine they followed religiously. "Wash on Monday, Iron on Tuesday, Mend on Wednesday, Clean on Thursday, Bake on Friday, Shop on Saturday and Rest on Sunday."

The Palmer's were members of Denvers high society. They wanted Rose to be aware of the arts and theater. They introduced her to books and plays at the Cheesman Park Pavilion and other social events in the city.

The Judge owned the Ogden Theater on Colfax and owned another theater. It may have been called the Bluebird.

After Rose completed her chores for the family, she would catch up on her letter writing and meet some friends at the park.

Soon the social season started, and Rose was very busy polishing silver and dusting off the good china in readiness for guests. The house had to be put in order, and she was instructed on how to greet the guests and her duties during the evening festivities.

Rose was enjoying her new status in life and time passed quickly for her. She should have graduated from South High School, but when she left the Frasiers that was the end of her schooling. She turned eighteen in March. The year was 1915. Janet married Ira McKeever in July.

Rose's life was good, and she was happy working for the Palmer's. The parties were starting at Easter that year and it was such an exciting time; the hustle and bustle of the city with horse and buggies and automobiles tooting their horns, people walking to and fro. Spring was always nice because the weather was warming up and it felt so good to be outside. The doors and windows were open to let in the fresh air.

There were several parties that summer, and there was also talk about the war in Europe and the Kaiser. It left a feeling of unrest and uncertainty among the eligible bachelors, although it would be a couple of years before America would get involved in the war.

Rose's friends had graduated in the early summer and had either gotten married or left town for more schooling or jobs. She was considered an attractive woman that made her popular with others her age. So it wasn't too surprising when one of the gentlemen at the Fall Fiesta, held at the Palmer's home, took a liking to Rose and made it a point to talk to her every chance he got. He watched to see when she went in the pantry to get more supplies and he could talk to her briefly, alone. He was older and much more debonair than the boys her age. Rosalie was naturally flattered at his flirting and his attention, but it made her feel funny to have him watch her so closely.

The Palmer's were very dependent on Rose. Since she had been with them, they thought of her like a member of the family.

The house was bustling with all the preparations for Christmas and the New Year Eve parties. The Palmer's had numerous friends, and they always looked forward to their parties. Of course Rose's attentive suitor was also a frequent guest at these parties, and she was worried that the Palmer's might be upset if they knew how interested he was in her.

The holidays passed and it was a new year, 1916. News from Janet was that she had lost her baby; she only carried it for a few months when she miscarried.

Rose had been emancipated from the orphanage when she turned eighteen; so she was free to come and go where she pleased.

Rose decided to visit Janet in Kit Carson. She told Janet she really wanted to go to Sedro Woolley and see their Grandmother Gillis, but she had no money, and begged Janet for the money for the trip. It was a hardship, but Janet and Ira gave Rose three hundred dollars.

CHAPTER 4

RETURN TO SEDRO WOOLLEY 1916

The train to Washington took several days and made many stops along the way. It is curious for Rose to take this train trip after her experiences the first time she was sent from her home. It was as though she was numb, she had no feelings one way or the other about being all alone and traveling in this manner. It was not usual for a young lady to travel alone in this time of unrest. Rosalie had lots of time to think.

She let her mind wander back to when she was a child. She remembered her Uncle Walter giving her a ride on his bicycle when she went to visit her Grandmother Gillis. She lived in Sperling just a few miles out of Sedro Wooley. Rosalie spent a lot of time at her grandmother's; her mother had her hands full with the babies, and she wasn't able to give Rose much attention. Janet was a lot of help to her mother, and she was always there if her mother needed something.

She remembered when they lived in Three Lakes and her father worked at the shingle mill. On Sundays they would take a picnic lunch, and the grownups would have a baseball game, and the children would run the logs on the river. How dangerous that was. They could have fallen and been crushed by the logs or drowned, but it was so much fun.

Rose couldn't remember seeing any police in the town of Three Lakes; as far as she knew, there was no official law and order. But there was a group called the Night Riders and if you were out after dark you could see them riding through town all dressed in black.

Everyone was afraid of them. The rumor around town was that they killed anyone that got in their way.

Rose was a tomboy, and she liked to do what the boys did instead of sitting and knitting. It was so much more fun to run the logs and slide down the chute into the pile of sawdust at the bottom. This one day when she decided to slide down the chute with the saw dust and land on the pile at the bottom, she came up coughing and could hardly breathe, she had so much sawdust in her lungs. Help came and took her home. The doctor said she was a very lucky girl to be alive. Even so she became so ill she nearly died. Her skin turned a real funny yellow color, as if it would rot. Eventually she got well and she learned her lesson about the dangers of sliding down on the sawdust. She would never do that again.

Shortly after that, her Momma got sick and had to go stay at Grandmother Gillis's. Three Lakes was about thirty miles from Sedro Woolley. The next few months they were back and forth from Three Lakes to Sedro Woolley; her father worked at the shingle mill from March to October. The family then moved to Sedro Woolley at the end of October to be closer to Momma.

That Christmas of 1908 was not a happy time for the family because Momma was so sick. But Rose remembered her Momma gave her an autograph book, with a red velvet cover for Christmas. She wrote on the inside front cover, "December 25, 1908, To my daughter Rosalie."

Rosalie remembers her grandmother sent her to town to fetch the doctor, but the consumption had gotten very bad. These thoughts made Rosalie very sad and sometimes she cried. Then she scolded herself and tried to concentrate on her journey.

The train was crossing the Rocky Mountains They were very beautiful and covered with snow. The trees were starting to look like the forests in Washington. She just let her mind wander and the warmth from the coal heater in the train car soon made her doze off.

When she awoke the train was crossing the Columbia River in

Oregon. The trip was tiring on her, and she was anxious to get to her grandmother's.

The closer she got to Sedro Woolley, the more she realized how much she had missed her grandmother. It had been seven years since her Momma had died. So much has happened to all of us.

I wonder where Ruth is? Poor Charles he never had a chance to have any happiness he was always so sick. I hope Joe is happy with the family who took him in. Brother John works so hard in the coal mine; he is sixteen now. I hope he can leave there and find a good job soon. I wonder what Poppa would have said if he had known what Joshua Clem did with all the money and the move to that barren prairie to live in a tent.

Finally the train was approaching the station at Sedro Wooley, Uncle Laurence was waiting for her. Everything looked so different, but it was January and when she left it was September. She tried to put it all out of her mind; the memories were rushing back as if it were yesterday. *I hope this wasn't a mistake coming back here.*

"Rose over here, it is good to see you. Mother couldn't bear to come to the station to meet you. She is waiting at the house, she is so anxious to see you," said Laurence.

Rosalie could hardly speak, tears welled up in her eyes and her throat was all choked up. She just stood there and let Uncle Laurence get her bags as she stumbled to the carriage.

Rosalie gained a little composure on the ride to Grandmother's and asked Laurence to fill her in on all that had happened since her Momma's death.

"I married Myrtle shortly after you left and we have a son, Emslie and a daughter, Viola. As far as any other news you will have to drag that out of your grandmother," said Laurence

Rosalie sat back and watched the countryside. She tried to find something familiar to let her know this wasn't just a dream to be here in a place that she could only remember as a child. It doesn't look like the same world. " I feel so old, I can't believe I was once a child here," she said to Laurence.

"A lot has happened to you, and I am sure it is hard to forget all the hardships you have been through," replied Laurence. "Here we are, you go on in and I will get your things."

Rose started up the steps to her grandmother's house and she heard her Grandmother's voice. "Oh, my dear, oh, my dear," said Grandma. "It is so good to see you, come in, come in. I hope the trip wasn't too tiring, are you hungry? Let me get you something to eat."

"I'm not very hungry, Grandma, I am just so glad to be here, can I have some water, please?" Rosalie was feeling kind of weak, she felt like her legs would collapse under her if she didn't sit down soon.

"Of course, my dear, here sit down I will get you some water. I will make a pot of coffee for later, after you have a chance to catch your breath. Now, tell me how is Janet?" asked Grandma

"Janet married Ira McKeever last July, and just a few months later she lost their baby. I haven't been to see her, but we write, and she said she was feeling much better and she was back on her feet right away after she lost the baby. She and Ira have so much to do she couldn't lie around in bed while Ira was working so hard to improve their ranch and make it livable. And Janet works so hard, fixing up the house," said Rose.

"Aunt Ida Bea's daughter, Lora, married John Wherry in Kit Carson, in December, just before I left to come visit you. Frantz and Wendell are working in Kit Carson. Without them Aunt Ida Bea would really be strapped; she still has four of her kids in school. The youngest is just eight years old. Janet writes me all the news about everything that goes on in Kit Carson," said Rosalie.

"Tell me about these people you are working for in Denver," asked Grandma.

"They are very nice people to work for, and I have my own room with some very nice furniture. But I was so home sick I thought it would be a good idea if I came to visit you for a while. They wanted to pay my way, but I wouldn't let them. They have done so much for me already," explained Rose. "I went to see Janet first.

Laurence came into the kitchen and said, "I will have a cup of coffee, then I have to run, Myrtle is waiting for me. After we get back from Vancouver, we are moving to Everett. I hope to find work there. Are you just here for a visit or are you moving back here to stay?"

"I don't know what I am going to do yet, I am so confused, I love it here , but there are so many memories I don't want to remember. While I am here I want to visit Momma and Poppas graves."

"We can do that tomorrow, I am sure you must be tired, go upstairs and freshen up and lie down for a nap, you will feel better after you have rested," said Grandma.

Rose didn't realize how tired she was. She fell asleep as soon as her head hit the pillow. When she awoke she felt much better and now she was hungry, she could smell something delicious drifting up the stairwell. She went into the kitchen and found Grandma cooking up something that smelled like soup and potatoes and onions.

"How was your nap, dear?" asked Grandma.

"Oh, it was wonderful. What are you cooking? It smells delicious," answered Rose.

"I made a beef stew, we will have plenty for supper tonight, too. I will have Viola and Emslie all the time when Laurence and Myrtle move to Everett. Emslie doesn't like to stay. Viola is six years old now and she spends more time with me than with her parents. Myrtle cries when she has to leave her. Laurence can't stand to be around her, and he wants Myrtle all to himself," said Grandma as she dished up a big bowl of stew for Rosalie.

Rosalie sat down to the table and enjoyed the warmth of the stew refreshing her body, as Grandma continued with the conversation about the two brothers differences.

"When Ernest comes to visit me and Viola is here, he really hits the ceiling. Viola is such a sweet child, I feel sorry for her. Ernest and Laurence can't be in the same house very long before they are arguing about the way Laurence treats the child," said

Grandma. "That's enough of that talk, let's talk about what you are going to do."

"I guess everyone has their problems, don't they, Grandma? We would get so tired and frightened when that horrible Joshua Clem would yell at Aunt Ida Bea; he treated her so badly. He didn't treat the rest of us very good either. I often wondered if Poppa knew how bad Clem really was. Maybe things would have been different if he had only known," said Rose.

"Don't torture yourself, dear, you can't go back and change anything, that is just the way it was meant to be. It's always best to leave well enough alone." said Grandma.

"I miss your Momma so much, sometimes at night I cry myself to sleep just thinking about her. It's been thirteen years since your Grandpa Gillis died and I still miss him, he was so young, too." .

"I remember Grandpa, he was such a tease, he couldn't do much but sit in his chair, but he sure liked to tease us kids. How old was he when he died?" asked Rosalie.

"He was only fifty-six, his legs bothered him so much, and his feet swelled up and hurt to walk on them, he would get blood clots and the doctor said that is probably what killed him," said Grandma

"Laurence, Myrtle and Viola are coming over to have dinner with us, would you like that?" asked Grandma.

"Oh, yes that would be very nice. I don't think I have ever met Aunt Myrtle," said Rose.

Your Aunt Rosalie will be so glad to see you. She has two boys, they are four and six. You were both named after your Great Aunt Rosalie, you know.

About that time Viola came running into the room, she was so glad to see her Grandma, "Mother, why do you let Viola run in the house?" said Laurence.

"You are the parent, Laurence, she is only a child. Hello, Myrtle, how are you feeling?" asked Grandma.

"I'm feeling pretty good today, thank you, but I'm not looking forward to going to Vancouver, that is such a tiring trip. You must be Rosalie, Laurence has told me so much about you, you are just as pretty as he said you were. I am pleased to meet you," said Aunt Myrtle.

"Thank you, I am pleased to meet you, also," Rose replied.

"Sit down, the table is set and the food is ready, I think our visitor is hungry, aren't you dear?" said Grandma.

"Yes, thank you, the food looks and smells delicious," said Rosalie

"What have you heard from Walter, Mother?" asked Laurence.

"I received a letter from him week before last, he enjoys working with the people of China. He said it is very rewarding, but the people live in such poverty, it is sad. He feels it was providence that sent him to China. He has much to learn. Nellie keeps busy helping the children and Ithiel is in boarding school in Seattle. Bernice attends school in Peking. She will be going to the same school as Ithiel in a few years," replied Grandma.

"I couldn't live that way," said Laurence. "There is always a war going on somewhere over there, and you never know when you will have to be evacuated."

"Uncle Walter sent me a book from China," said Viola, "and Momma read it to me."

"Viola, sit up straight and don't talk with food in your mouth," said Laurence.

"Yes, Poppa," answered Viola.

"How long are you going to stay, Rose?" asked Aunt Myrtle.

"I'm not sure, I was so home sick, I wanted to see Grandma, I missed her so much. I used to spend a lot of time with Grandma before Momma died," replied Rosalie.

"What in the world does one do in Kit Carson, Colorado and whatever possessed your Uncle to take you children there in the first place?" asked Aunt Myrtle.

"I am not sure, but he said he wanted to get free land and homestead it, but I think he just wanted Poppa's money," said Rose.

"Do you hear from your brothers?" asked Laurence.

"Janet and I hear from John, but since Joe is living with a family that may adopt him, we haven't heard from him for quite awhile," said Rose.

Rose's first evening at her Grandma's went by smoothly. Uncle Laurence and Aunt Myrtle left Viola with Grandma, as they were leaving for Vancouver in the morning. It was easier to leave her now than to bring her over in the morning on their way out.

The next day Grandma, Viola and Rose went to the cemetery to visit Momma and Poppa's graves. Uncle Albert and Grandpa were buried there, too.

Grandpa's headstone said John Alfred Gillis died May 12, 1903, he was 56. There was no headstone for Lydia Martella Reuter the cemetary records just showed the location of her grave. Now where was Joseph buried? There was no record of him being buried in this cemetary. Not too far away they found Uncle Albert's, it said Albert Arthur James Gillis, died March 7, 1902, he was only 30, just a year before Grandpa Gillis died. They put flowers on all the graves, then found a bench to take a rest. Rosalie felt nauseous. Why wasn't Poppa buried next to her Momma?

"I buried my second little girl, Victoria, in Quebec, she was only eight months old, she died January 29, 1880, then Ernest was born in August of the same year. I didn't have time to grieve for my little girl. I had two more babies after Ernest. Then we moved to Sedro Woolley in 1886. Your Mother was ten years old," said Grandma with tears in her eyes.

It was time to return to the house. Rosalie was very sad. "Grandma, why is there no headstone for Momma? Where is Poppa buried?"

"I think a cup of tea will taste so good when we get home, don't you?"

"I hope you still have some muffins, Grandma, that would really taste good with a cup of tea," said Viola.

"Yes, I have muffins and gooseberry jam. When was the last time you had gooseberry jam, Rose?" asked Grandma.

"I haven't had gooseberry jam or muffins since before Momma died. You make the best jam and muffins in the whole world, Grandma," replied Rose.

On the ride home they met some of Grandma's neighbors, and they passed the time of day with them. They were glad to see Rose again and asked about her brothers and sisters. It looked like it might rain, so they had to end their little chat, and hurried home before they got wet.

It felt good to be inside, but Rose couldn't shake the chill that she felt in the cemetary. Why won't grandma talk about where Poppa is buried? It was as if he wasn't to be mentioned again.

While they were having tea , there was a knock on the door. " Now who can that be?" said Grandma as she went to answer the door.

"Oh, hello Frank, How are you today?" asked Grandma.

"I am well, thank you, and you?" replied Frank

"I can tell it is going to rain because my knees are creaking," said Grandma. "Would you like to come in and meet my granddaughter Rose. She just arrived yesterday. We are having some tea, won't you join us?"

"I wouldn't want to intrude, but thank you for asking." said Frank.

"Not at all," said Grandma, as she ushered Frank into the parlor. "Frank this is my granddaughter, Rose, from Denver."

"Pleased to meet you, Miss," said Frank.

"Rose, this is Frank Moore, he works with Ernest, he is a carpenter, and he takes care of my flowers, when I can't bend down to pull the weeds. Frank, you know Viola of course." said Grandma. as she poured another cup of tea.

Little did Rose know, at this time, that this man would haunt her the rest of her life. This is the beginning of the secret that she is determined to take with her to her grave.

Emslie came in from playing and grabbed a muffin on his way out again.

Aunt Rosalie arrived before they finished their tea. "Oh, good

I was hoping I would get here in time for tea. It is so good to see you, little namesake, you look so grown up."

Rose gave her aunt a big hug and then started crying. It was just too much to see how much she resembled the way she remembered her momma before she got sick. After awhile the crying subsided and she was able to say how good it was to see her. They spent the rest of the afternoon catching up on old times, but the subject of where poppa was buried was always changed to talk about something else.

Rose felt sad but secure with her grandmother and the time passed quickly. Her freedom was short lived however, and in February Rose went through a horrible ordeal. In March she left suddenly for Denver.

Grandma Gillis heard from Laurence frequently after their move to Everett. It seems he was accused of mishandling some funds at his place of work and he could not get his boss to clear up the matter.

(letters printed from originals)

Everett, Wash.
March 1916

Dear Mother & All;Babies

Well I will write you and let you know I am still alive now. Momma I am about over my cold. I have gotten the best of it. The man I was working for got out of town before I got well and so I was beat again. Yes, Mamma, there is a great summer ahead of us and I am stuck here in Everett. It is a poor place to get work in. In Seattle there is lots of work on the employment boards. But I am here living from hand to mouth to get a start. I do not know why I write tonight, Saturday, as I do not have any idea you have a chance to get what I want. But I am going to ask anyway. I know I can work when I get the job and I tell you I need one too, of course it is like anything else. People do not believe me, but I tell you I can be ounest. And if you knew any was to try just once more to get $25.00 or $50.00 to give me a start. I tell I would work my hands off for you and babies. No matter what turned up, you could take a little to live on and send me the rest and I sure would work if I had to go anywhere. Everybody is here in Everett can't get work. But there is lots of it in Seattle. Now I tell you Mama, Mrs. Bingham would not miss that much and I sure would pay it back. I also would get my life insured so if I got sick or anything, she would get it anyhow. Things are awful here and I tell you I do not want to write without sending you some money, but what am I to do, just scrape and that is all I can get now. If I sent because I am lazy because there is not a bone in my body that is not sore thinking about you and what there is to face up there and I can not get work. I tell you here in Everett it is awful how things are and I am not coming home again till I can make good. I suppose babies ask for me, but it is not to them like it is to me. You know how it is as you can tell how it is to lose babies. Or what it is to a Father in the shape I am to leave all they have, all for a small mistake when they are nothing but a baby his self. But time will tell and when we get older we all can look back at our fate. But I am thankful I am still a man and will try to get to the top. Of course I can muster that. I would not worry you any but they are not so bad that some day I will make good and get on top. I will not trouble you with any more, only wish that some day while you are still able to enjoy life I can put a little money in your hand to let you know I will mean to repay you for what you have done for me. As there has been too many between and I tell you I never expect to tell you all I have to tell you, till I exceed in one thing. Then maybe you will look back a few years. I am now getting some more gray hair as I face this time of need for all of us. Things are day to day here and those that let their money go when they are wet. Hang on to it now and then there is no more. Well, Mamma take care of yourself and all. And if there is a way all right, if not, do not waste any more stamps till I can make good. because I am going to leave Everett if it has to be alone. But I tell you there is no use asking or writing to you as I have no heart without something to send you. Well I will close and I will stay till you have time to write. Then I have to do my best for some other way. But I think Mr. or Mrs. Bingham would do this for me and I will not sink anymore on anything but straight ounest work with my hands. I am still a good boy and all wright. And will still stay that way. But just a little foolish. That is all, But remember we have all our. Well I see Rosalie Reuter left for Colo. I see in a paper that was here at Tony's, but I do not read anymore. Tony us gone from here and his paper came here that is how I heard. Well I suppose you know, anyhow it is all right. Well bye for now. Love to all and babies. I am as ever your son, Laurence p.s. I have written over the amount, but I am still strong minded and you will excuse my over writing.

Oct 28, 1917
Dear Mother,

This is Monday, I went to Mt. Vernon and paid my note for $100.00. And I find out I have to have some more to make ends meet. So I may be able to get more but he would rather me have something that he could say I had. Now my place is worth $600.00 all right and no doubt I will be able to sell it, but there is $175.00 against it. Now I was thinking the Place up there is a house but it is not much the way it is and if it were to do some good I could get a deed from you without anyone up there knowing and put it with mine. It would be worth about $1000.00 all told. Then I would be able to say I was worth $1000.00. Then I could get money from time to time from the Bank and that way get by, of course, I would not sell that—by no means. Also I would only have it in name if I should sell mine then Deed it back to you. By that way it would do us both good. I am going to Anacortes tonight. I would come up but cannot at present Mr. Simmons at Mt Vernon will phone you when he gets the Deed. Signed by you and he will fix it up at Mt. Vernon and mail it to me. Now this is a onest propozition we made. We must get together and help one another. You have not got it listed with anyone have you? If you did I would burn it and give you the money. Well if you feel like it fix it up before the 1st so if I should like to get $100.00 on a note that would help me also give me a chance to pay the mortgage. Well I have about $50.00 standing out that is good but does not help at present. I will look for a letter tomorrow. Fill in blank and send to me or Simmons at Mt. Vernon. It is on the quiet, no one has anything on me or I do not hold any bills out—See/ Well by by for now, Laurence

CHAPTER 5

ROSE & JANET 1918

From this point on the story is built on speculation and some fact. The next two years are full of turmoil. Rose reveals that there was a Dr. Harbough who was named custodian of the children, after their father's death. Why he agreed with their father to send them to live with Uncle Joshua Clem is a mystery. There is only one statement of logic that Rosalie remembers and that is, *"in Canada, children and horses are always well taken care of first"*.

Dr. Harbaugh did not object when Joshua Clem decided to take the children to Colorado. It is believed that the Reuter Family Bible went with Anna Zimmerman Reuter to Colorado. The information in this Bible would hold some answers to many questions, although it may be recorded in German.

The children always remember that Bible sitting in the parlor and they were instructed to never touch that Bible. Hanging on the wall of the parlor was Grandfather's crossed swords and other paraphernalia from the Civil War.

Their Grandfather died in Ohio, 1903. He was in the Ohio Volunteer Infantry in the Union Army, 107th Co. K. He lost a leg some time after the war. They never saw any of the Civil War items nor the Bible ever again.

In reminiscing with her Grandma Gillis, Rose remembers how her Grandmother Reuter always called the children "Swine huntz", "Little Pigs", but never in front of their Momma.

When Momma got sick, Grandmother Reuter would do the cooking for the family. She would only cook German food and tell the children they had to eat every bite of food on their plates. She was not their favorite grandparent. She would speak her language to their Poppa so no one knew what she was saying.

Now back to Grandma Gillis. Rose was fitting into the routine of every day living. Grandma would save the used tea leaves, from all the tea they drank each day, and when it was dry, she would sprinkle it on the rugs and sweep it back and forth until it cleaned the rugs and then she would sweep it out the door onto the porch to be picked up. She said this was the way to clean the rugs until you could take them out to the clothes line to beat them.

A couple of months passed and Rosalie seemed to be enjoying the time spent with her Grandma. Her birthday was coming up soon, she would be nineteen on the 25th of March, 1916. Her Grandma planned a special dinner with cake for her. Since her Momma died, birthdays didn't mean much to Rose. She seemed to be numb to any thing that should have been fun.

Something terrible happened to Rosalie between February and March of that year. She wouldn't be celebrating her birthday. She told her Grandma she had to return to Denver immediately. Everything bad happened in Sedro, Woolley. When she boarded the train for Denver in March, there was no doubt that Rose was expecting a child.

It is unknown, if Grandma Gillis knew of this coming event. I think she did, and I also think that Aunt Rosalie knew.

Rose returned to Denver and went straight to the Palmer's. She obviously confided in them and told them everything that happened, or she made up a story. In any event this would be the beginning of deception that she would carry with her all the days of her life.

The Palmer's were very caring people, and they took her in and showed her all the compassion a person in her condition needed. When her time came to deliver, the Palmer's took her to Mercy Hospital. This was October 17, 1916. Judge Palmer took care of the birth certificate and made it look like Rose had been married.

The name on the certificate was baby Moore, but it was listed as not legitimate. This record was not accessible for many years.

Later, Rose named the baby Janet Shirley Moore.

Rose continued to work for the Palmer's. They gave her and the baby a home.

The Palmer's had a son and daughter, but so far they had no grandchildren. The Palmer's loved the little girl and became very attached to her. They were sad when Rosalie said she and the baby had to go to her sister's in Kit Carson. Rose got word that her sister Janet was very ill with the flu. The flu of 1917 to 1918 killed many people and she felt she needed to go to help her sister.

Mother Palmer told Rose that she would always have a home with her, and if she ever needed anything she could always come to her for help. Over the years Rose kept in touch with Mother Palmer and cleaned for her when she needed help. Rose was still helping Mother Palmer, Anna L. Palmer, when she died in 1944.

Rose and her baby, Shirley, boarded the train for Kit Carson. The war in Europe was causing people to be afraid. The Stock Market was shaky. There were lots of soldiers going to their bases, some were going home for Christmas. The train was bustling with travelers and the coach was crowded. Rose found a seat where the baby could lie down.

Rose had written to Janet that she would be arriving and was hoping some one could pick her up at the station.

When the train arrived in Kit Carson, one of the hired hands was there to meet her. Rose hadn't told Janet about the baby, but there were not that many young ladies getting off the train. He loaded Rose's things onto the buggy and helped her and the baby aboard.

When they got to the ranch, Rose was impressed at how the ranch looked. Not at all like the one where Joshua Clem dumped them.

Janet came out of the house carrying her baby. She had not heard from Rose for over a year and in the meantime Janet had given birth to her second child, named Johnny. Janet and Rose hugged each other so tight and crying at the same time. "Why didn't you tell me you were married?" said Janet.

"I'm not married. I heard you were deathly ill, and why didn't you tell me you were going to have another baby?" answered Rose.

"I was so sick I thought I would die, Ira said I was so delirious I didn't know who he was most of the time. Let's go in the house where we can talk and catch up on everything that has happened," said Janet.

It felt so good to be with her sister again. Rose was happy that Janet had a home of her own and that she had Ira, and now she has this new baby.

"This is Janet Shirley, she is just a year old," said Rose, "I call her Shirley."

"Let's get some supper on the table, I bet little Shirley is starving. You both must be very tired," said Janet.

After supper Ira went to check on his live stock and make sure the chickens were in. You had to be very careful not to scare up a rattlesnake. Some times they were in the nests when you went to gather the eggs.

Rose got Shirley ready for bed and she no sooner laid her in the bed than she dropped right off to sleep.

Rose went to help Janet clean up the supper dishes and finally have a chance to visit with her sister. "Have you heard from John, (he was always called Gillis before they went to Aunt Ida Beas') or Joe?" asked Rose.

"I got a letter from him, and he left the coal mine and joined the Army. He said he would let me know where he was when he finished boot camp. I haven't heard from Joe, though, I think he has run away from the foster family that took him last, it doesn't look like he will be adopted. He's only fifteen, so young to be on his own, but we have all been on our own for a long time now, I guess if we have made it this far, we can't be stopped now." said Janet.

"Now tell me about this man that you met and what is his name, and why aren't you married?" asked Janet.

"Oh, Janet it is so horrible I can't talk about it, I don't want to remember. I just want to put it out of my mind and never bring it up again," said Rose.

"But you have a daughter that will remind you of what happened every day of your life. All you have to do is look at her and you will remember," said Janet.

"You don't have to tell me that, but I don't ever want her to know what happened to me. The Palmer's don't even know everything, they were so good to take me in after this horrible deed. I feel so ashamed that I brought all this on the very people that have given me so much. They think the world of Shirley and felt so bad when we left. I couldn't stay there and cause them any more embarrassment. It is all my fault and I must carry this burden alone," said Rose.

"Did you visit Grandma Gillis in Washington like you said you would?" asked Janet "That was the last time I heard from you. I didn't know if some thing had happened to you or if you changed your mind."

"No, I didn't change my mind, I went, I now know that it was a big mistake. I never should have gone. It seems nothing I do ever turns out right." said Rose.

"You get some rest tonight and we will talk some more in the morning, you are tired and not in your right mind," said Janet as she lit a lamp for Rose to take to the bedroom.

"Take this lantern out side with you to the outdoor toilet, follow the path, remember how the rattlesnakes curl up in the sage brush at night." said Janet.

"I had forgotten, I was so lucky living in Denver; we had more luxuries there," said Rose.

The next morning Janet fixed breakfast for Ira, who had already been out to tend to the livestock since daybreak. Little Johnny was a good baby. Janet changed his diapers, nursed him and laid him in his cradle so she could tend to the morning duties, like building the fire in the cook stove, pumping water and preparing breakfast. While she was making the biscuits she was also preparing the bread for later in the day. This she did every morning.

Ira was having a cup of coffee when Rosalie came down from her bedroom with Shirley. "Good morning," said Rose.

"Good morning," said Janet and Ira at the same time.

"Ira just finished milking and I'll bet Shirley would like some cream on her oatmeal," said Janet as she fixed a bowl of oatmeal and a biscuit for Shirley. "How about a cup of coffee with your biscuits and gravy, Rose?" said Janet, not waiting for an answer.

The kitchen was warm and the food smelled so good, Rosalie hadn't realized how long it had been since she could enjoy a meal, but the numbness still consumed her and she wouldn't let her guard down, she might cry.

"We were so warm in that feather bed, neither one of us stirred all night, it was so cozy. I don't remember when I have slept so good."

Shirley was a quiet little girl and just ate her breakfast without saying a word. She could talk pretty good for a one year old, when she wanted to.

"I have to get to work, so I will see you later," said Ira, as he put on his hat and coat and went out the door.

Ira was born in Sharon, Kansas in 1887. He made his first trip to eastern Colorado when he was twenty-one. With wheat harvest over and desiring to become a rancher and leave the wheat fields, Ira rode on horseback to his uncle Walter McKeever's ranch ten miles north of Eads. On his next trip he came by train and walked the ten miles to his uncle's ranch. He was then ready to take up a homestead in 1911. It was about three miles south of the last McKeever residence and fifteen miles southeast of Kit Carson.

Ira was now 30 years old, eight years older than Janet, he was a foreman for the Thompson Ranch in Kit Carson. It was a large spread and they had a lot of cattle. Ira hoped he could build his little ranch up to be as big some day. It was good steady money working for the Thompson's and they were fair and honest.

He could make extra money when he shot a coyote and sold the hide, they brought $20 a hide, sometimes he had as many as five hides to sell. That was pretty good money. Nothing was easy in those days, though.

Rose helped Janet clean up the breakfast dishes and start preparing food for the next meal. Earlier Janet had made several loaves of bread and put them on the back of the stove to rise. By now the cook stove was good and hot and the oven was just right for the bread.

Janet took Shirley with her to gather eggs from the hen house, Shirley was a little frightened when the chickens flew all over when they walked in the hen house door. Janet was very good at reaching under the hens to gather the eggs, some of the hens never budged, they just clucked a little. The big old rooster was strutting around, he crowed and made a big ruckus when the sun came up.

The eggs were cleaned and stored in the cellar; it was so cool down there. Apples, potatoes, carrots and all sorts of home canned goods were on shelves and in bushel baskets; some of the things like onions were hanging from the ceiling. Ira would butcher a cow when they needed meat and Janet canned every thing she could get her hands on. They churned butter from the cream and made cottage cheese from the excess milk. The only thing they had to go into town for was flour, salt, beans and coffee, which wasn't very often. They had an ice box to keep some of the food cool during the day. An iceman had to deliver ice to them from town. There was a big ice house where they cut the ice in the winter from a nearby lake and covered it with straw to keep it from melting.

Janet put a beef roast in the oven when the bread was done and sat down to nurse baby Johnny. Finally Rose and Janet had a chance to sit down and finish their conversation from last night.

"Now, are you going to tell me what happened or are you going to make me imagine what happened?" said Janet.

"If I tell you, you have to promise me you will never tell another living soul, as long as you live. Promise?" said Rose.

"That isn't fair to make me make such a promise, but I promise you I will never tell. I will help you keep your secret," said Janet.

The two sisters talked and cried and Rosalie told Janet things that she could never have imagined. Now the two of them share the secret that can never be spoken.

Records of births, deaths, adoptions, marriages are not easy to obtain, especially in the early 1900's when they were sealed. It was not unusual for records to be falsified, so even if you were able to obtain any records, you couldn't be sure of their authenticity. Men have all the privileges and women carry the shame. The children, the other victims, suffered from the shame of being shunned by society.

Janet and Rose tended to the children, cleaned the house and washed the clothes on a scrub board. They had to carry water to the big round tubs and heat the water on a separate stove. They would then wring the clothes by hand and hang them out to dry on the clothes line, winter or summer. Sometimes when it was really freezing the clothes had to be hung inside and it made the house really steamy and took up a lot of space too.

Ira got home from work after dark and brought whatever mail they had from town. There was a letter from their brother John.

Supper was on the table when Ira arrived so he washed up and the three of them sat down to eat. Shirley sat on Rose's lap.

After supper Janet read the letter from John out loud. He had been sent to new Mexico for boot camp. He said it was a good thing he joined the Army when he did, because all the eligible men were being drafted into the Army, since war was getting closer to our shores. He said he lied about his age. You had to be eighteen to join up.

The summer was really hot and they made you hike for miles, the shoes wore blisters on your feet and you ached all over at the end of the day. The food wasn't bad, but the cots were narrow and uncomfortable. It looked like he would be sent to France as soon as he finished boot camp.

Not too many people had a radio, crystal set, so most of the news came from the talk in town or in the local paper.

Ira said there was a lot of talk about the War in Europe when he got the mail. Everyone is wondering who will get called next. He said some of the hired hands at the Thompson Ranch were getting worried if they would be going soon.

Janet continued reading John's letter, John was trying to locate Joe, but he wasn't having any luck. He wondered if she had heard from him. He also mentioned that he hadn't heard from Rose in a long time, either. He was concerned if she was all right. John said he wasn't sure if he would get any mail. If she wanted to write, she could send mail to the address on the envelope and hope he got it. He was sure glad to be out of the coal mine.

Janet went to the kitchen to dish up supper and set it on the table. Ira would eat and then go out to tend to the livestock and put them to bed. Rose helped Janet with baby Johnny. Shirley was such a good little girl, she liked to hold the baby, too.

Rose and Janet finished cleaning up after supper and put the babies to bed, then they sat down to do some mending. There was always work to be done, right up to bedtime, which was usually eight o'clock in the winter. The days started very early on the prairie. No one slept past five in the mornings, any morning, not even Sunday.

The next day Janet and Rose started planning the Thanksgiving Dinner, which was a week away.

Ira had asked some of the hired hands to share dinner with them and then go into town for the big dance they held every year. This was something to look forward to for Janet, since she rarely got to town to visit with the other farmers wives.

It was a small town and everyone knew everyone else. Rose wouldn't be a stranger; it had just been so long since she had seen some of her friends. Most of them were married now.

Janet said she had a dress that needed to be altered since she had had the baby. Rose had a dress that was suitable; she wore it at the Palmer's once or twice.

The sisters were kept busy with cooking, cleaning, washing clothes and tending to the babies. There was so much to do before the holiday was upon them.

Thanksgiving Eve was a very busy time, as all of them had to have a bath. Now bathing wasn't all that easy, the water was heated on the cook stove and the wash tub was placed in the middle of the kitchen floor, the kitchen was the warmest room in the house, so all bathes were taken there. The door to the living room was covered with a curtain which was closed to give each one some privacy.

The babies were easy to bathe; they could sit in the hand washing basin. All the water had to be carried from the pump to the stove. It took several buckets to fill the wash tub, not to mention the time it took to heat the water, and the kitchen wasn't available until after the evening meal. Washing your hair was quite an ordeal also. It wasn't too bad for Ira even though he had thick black hair, but the women had long thick hair. Hardly any woman had short hair, but they wore their hair in many different styles, some had braids, knots or French twists. Someone had to pour the rinse water over each one to get all the soap out. Bathing was not a daily ritual, you must have guessed by now. Daily bathing was done over a basin by the hand pump, and if you wanted warm water you heated some in the tea kettle. Ira was always clean shaven in spite of the inconvenience; however, there were no other conveniences in 1917, on the prairie, in Colorado.

Men had to work very hard in these days. They rode long distances on horseback, some drove buckboards to haul necessary materials for barns and other out buildings.

Women worked just as hard if not harder, hauling water, wringing out clothes and hanging them on the clothes lines, summer and winter, chopping wood for the fire and hauling it to the wood bin in the kitchen, tending to the garden and canning everything they grew. They worked from before sun up to bedtime.

Janet enjoyed having Rose stay with them not only for her company, but also to share the work. They got a lot of visiting in while working.

Everyone was up bright and early on Thanksgiving Day, as usual, feeding and dressing the babies, breakfast was biscuits and gravy, bacon and eggs, jam and coffee, every morning.

Ira had shot a wild turkey the day before, so it had to be cleaned and feathered immediately and kept cool until the next morning when Janet made the dressing and stuffed it in the turkey, placed it in the oven and started the dinner while she was making the breakfast. Keeping things cool in the winter wasn't too difficult, as long as they had an early winter, but if the days stayed warm up until Christmas they had to store the perishables in the cellar with cool wet cloths covering them. Of course, the nights were very cool.

Whenever Janet wanted to cook chicken for dinner, the chicken was caught, killed, gutted, feathered, cleaned, and cut up less than an hour before it was cooked.

Some of the hired hands began to arrive for dinner, some were married and brought their wives and some were bachelors. Each one brought a pie or a cake for dessert. Janet was always grateful when they were so thoughtful to bring their specialty to share.

If the weather was nice, the men stayed on the porch to smoke a pipe or roll their own cigarettes and talk men talk.

All the women went to the kitchen to help get the food on the table. Rose was busy helping with the babies and doing what she could to set the table, with a clean starched table cloth and napkins. The table was huge; it would seat 12 people easily. A heavy oak table with thick legs and at least three leaves when extended full length, it took up most of the room that was just off the kitchen. Every farm house had to have a room like that, because you never knew when you would have to feed all the help during harvesting.

Three of the hired hands were married and three were single. Rose happened to sit across from the hired hand that picked her up in town. He had been eyeing her ever since he arrived. He couldn't take his eyes off of her. Rose was a little uneasy with all this attention.

Everyone had introduced themselves when they arrived and this one in particular was named Hank Kirby. His family lived in Eads, thirty miles south of Kit Carson. He had been driving cattle from Texas to Montana since he was fourteen. Now he was 21 and came back to find work closer to home. He had a fight with his father when he was fourteen and left home, joining up with the cattle drive. He wasn't anxious to see his father again soon.

After the meal they all headed for town, some on horse back and others on the buckboard. Shirley and baby Johnny were all bundled up for the ride to town.

The Town Hall was aglow with lanterns and there was a big fire going in the pot-bellied stove. The Fiddlers were warming up their fiddles and the whole town was mingling around getting acquainted and catching up on all the gossip.

Why, there must have been 75 people, men, women and children, at the gathering. Chairs were set up around the walls of the big Hall. There was a small stage at one end where the fiddlers set up their music.

Lora and John Wherry came over to talk to Rose and Janet. Their baby was just three months old. They talked about the babies, and asked about Rose's stay with the Palmer's. They were about to ask where her husband was when the Ramsey's came over to welcome Rose back. The Paul Meier's greeted Janet and Rose warmly and made small talk with the babies.

The men had been mingling outside smoking and drinking. Whiskey was passed around at these gatherings and most all the families had a bottle at home; you never knew when you might need it for medicinal purposes.

The fiddlers were all warmed up and ready to start the dancing. Hank asked Rose to dance before anyone else could. Soon the floor was crowded with the dancers. The children played wherever they could find a place to be out of the way. The women took turns taking care of the babies.

It was late when the dance broke up. Everyone was so tired; it had been a busy and long day. Everyone went their separate ways, the hired hands went back to the bunk house at the Thompson Ranch.

The Thompson's had their buckboard loaded up and took off for the ranch. Ira, Janet, Rosalie and two very sleepy babies climbed onto the buckboard and headed for home, down that rough and dusty dirt road.

Things returned to normal for awhile after Thanksgiving. Winter came on with a vengeance; only on the prairie can you experience high winds and drifting snow so high that it almost covered the house. Ira moved the livestock closer to the house before the winter took over. He made a path to the chicken house and the barn through the snow. Then he made a path to the out house with a rope tied from the house to the out house so you wouldn't lose your way in a blizzard.

Each bedroom had a commode under the bed so there was no need to go to the out house at night. The stories they would tell about someone getting up at night and going outside, wandering around in their night gowns trying to find their way back to the house, sometimes almost freezing to death. They would have to build up the fire and bundle up until they thawed.

Christmas was coming and no one had a lot of money. But most gifts were made, and the women got together for sewing bees and quilting. They knitted socks and gloves and hats besides sweaters. Most of their time was taken up with babies and children's clothes.

The fanciest doilies were crocheted and then starched as hard as porcelain. The hard winters on the prairie isolated women and they kept very busy looking forward to the occasional get-togethers in town. The men had to tend to the livestock, and they always had to sit or stand around the pot-bellied stove at the country store, chewing tobacco and smoking their pipes. Their conversations were called chewing the fat.

There was a lot of talk about the crop prices and how much they got for their cattle when they took them to market in the fall.

Hank managed to get invited to the house for supper pretty often, since he met Rosalie at the Thanksgiving festivities. Some of the other hired hands were teasing him about being "sweet" on Rose.

Janet and Rose were busy catching up on each others lives after they were separated.

"Aunt Ida Bea is still out at the dugout," said Janet, "She will come over for Christmas, with her three youngest."

"Where is Frantz, now? And Wendell?" asked Rose.

"Frantz went to Kansas as soon as he finished school, Uncle Joshua turned up in Fort Scott, Kansas, after he was run out of town, so Frantz wanted to go live with him." explained Janet, "Wendell took off for Arkansas as soon as he turned seventeen, I think he went to Bentonville."

"Are Lora and John Wherry coming to dinner, also?" asked Rose.

"Yes, Lora has a little boy and is expecting another baby in a few months. They are such a happy couple, I have always enjoyed visiting with them. John is a hard worker and he is so good to Lora." said Janet.

"I have missed Lora so much, she was my best friend when we were living in the tent that Uncle Joshua made us put up. It will be good to see her again, I didn't get to talk to her much at Thanksgiving," said Rose.

"Poor, Poppa, if he had only known what he was putting us through, I think he must be turning over in his grave." reminisced Janet. "I never told you this before, because I felt you were upset enough when Momma died, but when Poppa got word that we had arrived safely in Sault Ste Marie, with Aunt Ida Bea, he ripped his stomach stitches out, because he was in so much pain, from the cancer. He then died very quickly. Aunt Ida Bea only told me, she had to tell someone, she couldn't bear her grief any more alone,"

"I didn't know he had cancer, I thought he died of consumption like Momma. Oh, how much more of this can I take. Will things ever get better?" cried Rose.

"Try not to be too upset over this news, there is so much more I need to tell you. Dr. Harbaugh took everything Poppa had left. He only gave some of the money to Uncle Joshua to keep him quiet. Believe me he got his share of the money, too." consoled Janet. "Aunt Ida Bea tried to track down the family Bible, but Dr. Harbaugh said he didn't know what happened to it."

"Grandma Gillis didn't say anything about Dr. Harbaugh while I was visiting her," said Rose.

"Don't expect anyone to acknowledge that they know anything about Poppa's belongings, no one is talking. They are going to take what they know to their graves,"said Janet.

"By the way, does Hank think your husband died?" asked Janet. "Does he know that Shirley is your daughter?"

"Yes, I told him her father died before she was born. I told him you and Ira might adopt her, since I have no way of raising her by myself. Would you adopt her, Janet?" pleaded Rosalie.

"Why of course we would, but you can stay here with us as long as you need to, Rose, you know that. Shirley is a dear, and I have gotten attached to her already in just a short time, she loves baby Johnny and is so good to him. You need to take your time and not rush into any final decision too soon. Ira just loves children, and he teases Shirley. She likes him too." answered Janet

"I don't know what else to do, but I want to stay here for awhile, I feel so safe here," said Rose.

Christmas passed and the winter was tiring, deep snow drifts everywhere. When the wind blew it covered up the chicken house and covered the paths to the barn and the out house. But inside the house things went on as usual, baking, cleaning, washing clothes, ironing and sitting by the table into the evening keeping each other company. The house was steamy on laundry day and the aroma of coffee was always present. Ira would bring in armloads of firewood and the kitchen stove was always hot. The pot-bellied stove in the parlor was kept aglow all day, but at night you heated up some flat rocks and wrapped them in a towel to take to bed with you to keep your feet warm.

The beds were feather beds and heavy comforters covered you. By morning you were just as snug as a bug. You didn't want to get out of bed because you knew the floor was going to be ice cold and you would have to run to the kitchen to stay warm.

Soon it would be spring and the cows would be calving. Sometimes a calf would be born too early, and Ira would have to bring it in closer to the house so he can keep an eye on it. A rancher can't afford to lose a single animal.

The world outside of Kit Carson was in turmoil, and more and more young men were being called to join the Army. If you didn't join by a certain date you were drafted.

One day the skies were blue and the weather had cleared. It was bitter cold and the roads frozen hard. Hank arrived at the house to talk to Ira. He really wanted to see Rose, but he didn't want to be rude.

Hank was sitting in the kitchen drinking coffee with Ira, Janet was busy making bread, and Rose was ironing. Janet gave Shirley a wad of dough to let her make a small loaf of bread and Johnny was sitting on the floor on a blanket playing with a rattle made from a gourd.

"I got my draft notice in the mail. It looks like I have to leave June twenty sixth. They are sending the men to New Mexico for boot camp," said Hank

"I didn't think it would be long before you would be called," said Ira. "It seems like the war is getting worse not better. They will probably send you to France as soon as you finish boot camp. The President said all those eighteen and older would be called first, then if needed they would have to call those over twenty-five."

"Ira I hope they don't call you, you are already almost thirty," said Janet

"Single men first, then married, then married with children will go in that order. Some men are enlisting because they don't have a job and no hopes of getting one, so they figure they will be better off in the Army.

"I wonder if John has been sent to France yet?" said Rose. "We haven't heard from him in a long time. I sent him a letter before Thanksgiving and haven't heard a word back."

"These are just terrible times, how will some of these people manage, if there is no one to run the ranch. We will all have to help where we can," said Janet

March arrived along with Janet and Rose's birthdays, the 17th and the 25th, Janet was 23 and Rose was 21. Hank had supper with them for their birthday. Nothing special, just the regular food they always ate.

Hank had a chance to talk to Rose alone after supper. "I'm going to be leaving in two months and I don't know when I will be back, but I want to know if you will marry me before I leave?" nervously turning his hat in his hands.

"Why would you want to marry me? I have a child already. There are lots of girls you could marry," answered Rose.

"I am just a cowboy, most women don't want to marry a cowboy. Besides, I don't mind that you have Shirley, she is real cute and a very good little girl. I want to know that someone will be waiting for me when I come home, and there will be two of you. The first time I saw you I said, *I'm going to marry that woman*, I liked you right away," said Hank.

Rose started crying, she didn't know what to say. She could stay with Janet and Ira while Hank was gone and maybe she won't have to give Shirley to Janet after all.

She knew she had to answer Hank, but was it fair to marry him just to have a home for her baby? Did she really love him or just like him? Should she tell him the truth about Shirley or just let him think it is the way she said?

"I have to have some time to think about this, Hank, I will let you know before too long. I can't give you an answer right now. What if you don't come back from the war?" asked Rosalie.

"I will give you my Army pay while I am gone and you can save it for us, then we can get our own place when I get out of the Army. I have 160 acres in Eads my Dad said was mine when I get enough money to run it. I put away most of my pay now, but I still don't have enough to buy my own cattle yet. I'll be damned if I will take anything from my Dad if I can't run it myself," said Hank.

"Will you go with me to Eads as soon as it warms up? I want you to meet my family," asked Hank.

"I will let you know in a few days," said Rose

Rose was so confused now, what was she to do? I will have to talk to Janet, thought Rose.

Rose and Janet sat up and talked, after they put the babies to bed.

"Janet, what should I do? Hank wants me to go to meet his family and he wants to marry me. Now what am I going to do?" asked Rose.

"What about Shirley?" asked Janet.

"He wants her, too," said Rose

"When does he want to marry you?" asked Janet

"Before he goes to Boot Camp," replied Rose

"I don't know what to tell you, do you love him enough to marry him?" asked Janet

"I don't know how I feel, I know that I am grateful to him for giving me a way to keep my baby. I was in love with a man at the Palmer's, before I went to visit Grandma Gillis, but after what happened, I can never see him again. He doesn't know where I am, and the Palmers promised not to tell him about Shirley or where I am. I have made a complete mess of my life. Now I have a chance to make a home for a man I don't even love," rambled Rosalie.

"You have Shirley and she deserves to have a father, Hank did not ask you to give up Shirley. That says a lot for a man, that he cares for both of you," scolded Janet.

Rose and Shirley went with Hank to visit his family one Sunday. Rose was very nervous meeting his mother and father. Hank did not get along well with his father, at all. His mother was an outspoken woman, no one argued with her.

"Mother, this is Rose. I am going to marry her," said Hank. Rose this is my mother, Carrie."

"Where did the baby come from, whose is it?" asked Carrie.

"This is Shirley. Rose's husband died before she was born," answered Hank.

"Are you going to get married when you get back from the war?" asked Carrie

"No, we are getting married as soon as possible, before I have to leave," said Hank.

Sunday dinner went on as usual, getting to know the new additions to the family. Hank's brothers teased him and had plenty of advice to give him on marriage.

Rose was grateful when they left, she wasn't sure they had really accepted her and Shirley.

"I want you to have my Army Life Insurance in case I don't come back," said Hank.

"I can't accept that," said Rose.

"I want you to have it, not my Dad," insisted Hank.

Rose and Hank were married on June 25. Hank left for the Army the next day.

Rose helped Janet with the garden and the chickens, and part of the time she would spend time with Hanks family in Eads. The Palmers wanted her to come to Denver to stay while Hank was in the Army.

Rose decided to go to Denver for a visit so the Palmers could see how Shirley had grown.

Rose wrote to Hank every day, and he wrote as often as he could. But his mail would come in bunches, some days nothing. Part of the time he was in New Mexico; then he was sent to New Jersey for more training.

Hank and some of the others in his camp got the flu and were in sick bay for a week. Shortly after Christmas his troop was sent to France on the USS PRETORIA.

Rose managed to stay in Denver with the Palmers all winter. She returned to Kit Carson in May. The war had ended in Europe and the troops were sent home for discharge in June. Hank arrived in Kit Carson June 25th, exactly one year after he was inducted into the Army.

CHAPTER 6

WAR AND DEPRESSION 1919

Hank was never so happy to see solid ground and the prairie; he would not leave this country again. He told stories of the boat ride over and the mud and frozen trenches. He said the enemy was using mustard gas and it made some of the soldiers really sick. He said he was lucky, he came back all in one piece. But some of his buddies were injured badly, and some didn't make it back alive.

Hank and Rose set up housekeeping on the section of land between Eads and Kit Carson. Hank went back to work for Port Thompson. The Thompson ranch was huge, spread out from Eads to Hugo.

It was lonely for Rose and Shirley living in the one room soddy while Hank was riding the range, but every Sunday they were expected to have dinner with Hank's family. All of Hank's brothers and sisters families would be there also. The women cooked and gossiped, and the men smoked and chewed tobacco. Sometimes they discussed crops and the neighbors on the adjoining section with the latest farm equipment.

Eads
Nov. 16, 1919

Dear Sweet Hart Rose,
I got your letters one today and one yesterday I was sure glad to hear from you and glad you got the money.
Sweet Hart I would love to see you but I hate to think of bringing you home in this cold house untill I get some coal and get the heating

stove up. I will get some coal as soon as I can. I hate ask Bob for more money now.

    Mart hasn't shiped my stear yet but they are going to ship another load and he will ship him then. Sweet hart I got a sack of flower the other day. I have been making biscuits. If I get to much bread It dryes out so quick and gets hard. Sweet Hart take good care of yourself and babe. I have got a bad cold to. I swalowed some menthalatum last nite and rubed some on my throat and it helped me to.

    They have taken all of the stears up in the sand hills so there is nothing here but the calves and a few invlads. But I have to feed them every day. So when I come after you we will have to come back the same day. Roy came down with me last nite and helped me round up the calves and feed them.

    He was riding a bronk. He sure made him ride to he bent his spurs all out of shape and pulled leather with both hands.

    Say sweet hart did you hear about Hary York? His horse bucked with him and the saddle turned and the horse kicked him and drug him almost to death. He was unconcus for a long time. They took him to town and put him to bed and he is there yet. I heard today that he was getting along pretty well.

    Well sweet hart I would like to write a dozen pages but I can't think of any more to write. Besides I haven't had any supper yet and haven't got the fire made and it is 7 oclock. I think I done pretty well don't you? Well sweet hart good bye. I will come as soon as can. loving lines from Hank

    P.S. I didn' tell you we only got 231 head diped. we just started in the afternoon before the storm and the cattle all went to the ditch country and the vat froze and busted. Hard Luck. well, goodnite sweert hart I can almost see you. by by

    P.S. I thought of you all nite last nite and didn't sleep a wink. But don't worry sweet hart. I don't . This is almost a love letter sweet hart I can't quit. I know you like to read long ones though. Well good nite sweet hart sleep good.

    The winters were harsh, and you could be isolated for days after blowing snow and drifts. The farm hands would try to round up cattle and get them to some sort of shelter and food, but many cattle died during the blizzards. If you were caught in a blizzard, you went to the nearest farm and they would always take you in. During the long winters Rose would try to make the sod house as comfortable as possible. She would arrange the orange crates and cover them with cheesecloth to put the kerosene lamps on. One day as she was going through a saddle bag that Hank had kept with him where ever he went, she found some letters tied up with a piece of leather. In the letters were some interesting facts about Hank's life before she knew him.

There was a letter from his brother Dan.

Eads, Colo.
June 13, 1913

Dear Brother,
I received your letter Saturday. I don't think I can come down very soon, think I will go over to Ed Hickmans to look at a Bronk. He said he had forty head that I could take my pick out of. I'm going to try to trade a cow or a yearling heifer. I ordered me a pair of spurs from R. T. Frasier. If I get one and can't ride it will you ride it for me? Do you want to sell your old saddle? Millard Wetherman said he would give you ten dollars for it, but meby you could get twelve or fifteen for it. We have got another nester over east a mile and a half, his name is James, he wants a horse and saddle. Mart has been trying to sell him old Kim, he has got a cycle. Mart has been trying to trade him old Kim for the bicycle and twenty dollars, but he wont trade. Mebey you could sell your saddle for fifteen dollars to him. Have you got your horse with you? When I get my new spurs I'm going to practice riding steers.

from Dan Kirby

The next letter
Eads, Colo
April 10, 1914

Dear Brother,
Glad to now that you are back in Montana. Was it very cold in

Canada when you was there? It has been pretty good winter here this winter, but it was cold enough. There wasn't very much snow. Ehorst is going to run part of his cattle on the Starks place this summer and part of them here. There are two new mange inspectors here now and everybody has to dip their cattle now. We have been working Ted Now. Dall has got the black horse under the collar. Well I guess Bill and Lena get along all right, they bought another house and moved it up to the other one. They don't live the same place the little shack was. They moved further north by the middle mill. They have dug a well and got water and have got a windmill up. Fred Eders have got another boy. Did you now that George Eder had to be operated on for appendicitis, but he is all right now. School was out about a month ago and Womacks have gone to Kansas all but Lee, he's sticking around yet. Hightowers have got an automobile they go to town about every day. There was a dance at Spuergeons last Friday night. There was a big crowd there. Willeys and their relations were out from town and Fay Hinz and Oscar York. Old Jim Eage and Spuergeon furnished the music. John Lee is back, he is drunk half the time. Mannons east of here are going to leave in the fall. Pap rented their place and I guess he bought their cows.

from
Dan Kirby

And another letter.
Eads, Colo first day, Feburary
1915

Hello Hank,
How is Montana? Is it very cold there and what are you doing now? I am going to school but there ain't very big school. Dewey don't go. Dall got married a while back. He married one of the Camels girls they live on the Maning place. Manning has gone to Kansas. And Clay got married they are back in Kansas. He married one of the Millers girls. I got a horse. He is black. I have rode him four or five times. So I have got an outfit. Horse, saddle, blanquet and bridle. I got him from McDaniels the school teacher. He is one of the colts from one of them black mares that McDaniels bought from Port Thompson. *from Dan Kirby*

Rose made it a point to remember to ask Hank who Dan was and why she had never met him?

When Hank returned from Kansas he told Rose that Dan was his younger brother and he died when he was seventeen. Hank was in Montana and never knew what he died of, his mother never mentioned his death after the funeral.

The last letter Rose read from the saddle bag puzzled her even more, and Hank told her no one was to mention his brother's death.

Plain View Ranch
Nov. 20, 1915

Dear Hank,
    Will has gone for a load of feed at the Pyle's place. He has been hauling for quite a while but has not hardly got started yet. He sold some feed to Ehorst and he hauled that all to the Stark place. There was sixty seven head (I believe Will said) of Thompson Cattle in the Pyle's field all one day and one night so you know they got a good fill of corn and feed. Will drove them out the next morning when he went for feed. He sent them south and they were so full they could hardly walk. We had a big wind storm and that drifted them down there. They tore the whole north side of the fence down.

Dan just got back yesterday from another trip with cattle. He has been working for Belche, I think. I don't know if he went to Sugar City this time or not. He was gone a week or more. Papa didn't like it because he went, he wanted him to be shucking corn.

Did you know the folks had a new buggy? They had better get a Ford Car we think. Everybody around here had a Ford, they don't call them automobiles, just a Ford.

Mart, he does about as he pleases at home now. You know he is boss. Sometimes he goes to school and other days he don't. He goes to town when he gets ready and sometimes goes up to Sunday School. Just has a big time in general.

I got the pictures and think the one is just fine. You ought to send one to Grandma. You know it would tickle her so much and she thinks just as much of you as the rest of us. I could send her one of mine, but I don't think the one is very good, it is shaded too much.

Clay's address is Grantville. He is working for Shirleys. He did work for Wolfe's for sometime after he was married, but they have moved to Grantville now. I just got a letter from him the other day. You know Lou Wolfe has a store at Newman now and Clay was telling about him being fined Five Hundred Dollars for cheating in weight in the store.

Mary sent us one of her baby's pictures a short time ago, it is very cute. I think it looks very much like Lib's kid picture that is taken with you.

We are all invited over to Dall's for a turkey dinner, Thanksgiving. Don't you wish you would be here? Just for a little while anyway?

We were down to the folks last Sunday for dinner. I rode Kit down bareback and rode on a gallop too. What do you know about that?

The men were separating the cattle. They took in a hundred and twelve head to pasture. Lib and Harve drove in their dinky Metz buzz car when we had dinner ready to eat. They got Belche's old car. It looks pretty good, tho since they painted it up and it runs. They say that's all that is necessary.

I started to clean house the other day and land how the wind did blow! But I got the south room cleaned anyway. Will thought the wind blew in more dirt than I got out, but it didn't. I believe it is going to blow again today. If it does, Will can't haul feed so we will go to town.

The menfolks all went to Lamar last week one day to a land trial. Hightower's contested McHargue's place. You know by the folks east mill? That little white house. Will, and Fred, Pa, John Lee, Dall, Henry, Spurgeon, Fluke, Laura Maile, Hightower's and McHargue all went down. They don't know yet who beat. We all think that Mr. McHargue did tho.

I must get to work have not washed the dishes yet.

Lovingly your
sister Lena Pearcey
(don't forget how to spell it)

Dan died in 1915, no record of his death or month.

***

Hank would bring canned goods from Janet and Ira's well stocked cellar to Rose every time he was able to get home. They had not built up a supply in the short time they were homesteading. Many times they would go to bed hungry.

The next time Rose went to town, she and Janet caught up on the latest news. Janet could tell that Rose was soon to give birth.

"You should come home with me and stay until the baby comes," said Janet. "It's not good to be out on the prairie by yourself in your delicate situation."

In the mail was a letter from their brother Joe, they could hardly wait to read it.

Sedalia, Colo.
April 2, 1920

Dear Sis,
   How are you all?
   I quit Bush's Tue. night and 1 hr. later I had a job at $35 a mo.
   I was treated like a dog by Mrs. Bush and the kids so I decided to quit. I liked Mr. Bush.
   I don't think the home will do anything. The fellow I work for now is going to give me $50 a mo. starting next mo.
   This is a cattle ranch and we don't milk. It's right in the mts.
   Joseph J. Reuter
   Box 77

23rd of April Rose went into labor. Mrs. Ramsey was there to help Janet during the birthing. After several hours of labor, Doris was born. The doctor arrived soon after.

Meisenheim, Germany
May 20, 1920

Dear Sister Rosalie,

    Received your most welcome letter today and was very glad to hear from you. How are you feeling now? I am in the best of health at present and hope to remain so. I sure do wish to be back to see my nieces and nephew and I bet they sure are pretty if they take after their mothers.

    Rosalie I am afraid I am going to stay in the Army for a few years or at least with the Government Geological Survey as I think that is the best way I can get real good at Engineering and that I consider one of the best occupations there is. All the Master Engineers that I have worked for tell me to keep at the work as they think I will make good at it.

    I will be a Corporal next month and that is doing pretty good as all the others that are Corporals are re-enlisted men and as about all the Company are old men in the service, it is pretty hard for a recruit to advance much but most ot the men's time is up in five or six months and then there will be more vaccancies. I am working at present in the Company office working there in the morning and going to Surveying School in the afternoons so I do not have any drilling, Guard or K.P. and get a pass whenever I want it. If I was stationed some where in Colo. I could get a pass about every week or so and run down and see all of you folks. But when I do get back I will be able to get fourteen or 21 days leave every three months.

    Well I must close for this time. With Love, John
Ad. John G. Reuter A.P.O. 9270
Co. D 1st Engineers 2nd Brigade
A.F.I. Meisenheim, Germany

Lacross, Kans.
June 26, 1920

Dear Rose,

    This is Sunday. Clay and I are going to Sunday School with Lester Miller they talked us into the notion of going. It is only 1/2 mile to town.

    Well we started to harvest Friday after noon. We will get 7 dollars a day and a long job thrashing after harvest. How are you getting along with Louie? I hope you can stick it out till I get back.

I think I can make quite a sale. I guess Clay is not going to write. The first time I wrote to you I asked him if he wanted to write some and he said no you can tell them all the news.

We had a big rain here Friday nite but didn't stop harvest. Well I guess that will be all for this time. I think I told you about the fire in the other letter. Good-bye

I am your love, Hank

La Cross, Kans.
June 23

Dear Rose,

We got here Tuesday nite at 8 oclock. The roads were a frite. The last 40 miles. Harvest wont start before Monday here. We are both working for Miller. They are nice people. There was a house burned down right here close to nite. Just about 3 hundred yds from Millers house. Don't know what started it. Just went up in smoke all at once.

I don't know what the wages will be yet. Will tell you in the next letter. Be careful about fire. love from Hank

LaCross Kansas
July 1, 1920

Dear Rose,

I got your letter the other day was glad to get it to. we have been away for a week on the other place and haven't had time to write. Well my back is all write I am standing it fine. Well good bye I will write more the next time. love from Hank

Colby, Kans.
July 18, 1920

Dear Rose,

I am sending the films today this is Sunday and we don't have to work. We went to town last nite in a big Cale 8 it is sure a peach to.

Clay and I are going to Colby today to see about getting some trucks to haul wheat with. If we can get the trucks we can pay for them in about to months. They are paying 30 and 40 dollars a day for trucks and that looks good to us.

But don't say anything to any body about it for Pop will sure raise cane about us buying them. We have worked 6 days all ready and have got about two weeks yet.

I think this is the third letter I have wrote since I have been here and haven't got any yet but I know it not your fault the mail has to go so far around to get here. Well sweet hart we are ready to go to town. so good by. love from Hank R.R. 2 C.D. Pabst

Colby, Kans.
July 12, 1920

R.R. 2. C.D. Pabst
Dear Rose,
This is Sunday nite we got here this evening and got a job. The whole crew that worked for Miller at LaCross. The man we are working for has got 6 hundred acres of wheat so we will have a good long job.

I only got $73.50 at La Cross, was going to send you some money but didn't want to put any money in the letter. I will send you some the next time I go to town.

Say sweet hart I forgot to get them films but I will get them to you the next time I go to town. Well sweet hart it is so dark I can hardly see what I am writing so I will have to ring off. Best love from Hank

La Cross, Kans.
July 6, 1920

Dear Rose,
I got your letter Sunday and the shirts it just hapened that mine were both dirty. Well we had a big rain last nite. Clay and I were up town and had to wait till the rain was over. The rain didn't stop harvest we have worked every day except Sundays. Well we will be done harvesting in about three days.

Say sweet hart we have decided to go north for more harvesting and not do any threshing here. They only pay 6 dollars a day and we can get 7 in the harvest and it is not so hard work. I think we will go to Colby Kans. that is about 150 miles north west of here and come home from there. I will only have about 75 Dollars when I get done here and would like to make more if I can. I will send you some money as soon as I get paid.

Well sweet hart I guess that is all I have to say this time. Write soon as you get this letter and then wait till I write to you for we may be gone. Good bye sweet hart. love from Hank

Brewster, Kans.
Aug. 2, 1920

Dear Rose,

We got here this morning and went on to Colby, didn't strike anything there so we came back here and got a job threshing $7 a day. We were going back to Burlington, Colo and get a job harvesting, that is 35 miles north of Sheyen Wells but we got this job and we stoped. The old hoopey stoped on us at Goodland last nite and we worked on it for 2 hours. Well sweet hart I will close for this time and tell you more the next time. by from Hank

    Rose stayed with Janet until Hank was able to take her, the baby and Shirley back to the soddy. The worst wasn't over yet. The weather was unmerciful with wet snow and heavy rains flooding the washes and the waddies. Mud was knee deep.

    Hanks brother Clay was going on the harvest with Hank and his wife Louie stayed with Rose while they were gone.

    Finally the mud dried up and Rose tried to salvage the garden, clean out the soddy, wash the bedding and hang it out to air. Shirley helped her by watching the baby.

    Rose was just getting on her feet after the birth of Doris and it wouldn't be long until Janet was due to give birth. Shirley liked staying with Janet and Johnny was her close companion. She missed playing with her cousin when they would go to the soddie.

If it weren't for the mail life would be unbearable. It was always good to hear from their brother John.

Meisenheim, Germany
May 20, 1920

Dear Sister Rosalie,
    Received your most welcome letter today and was very glad to hear from you. How are you feeling now? I am in the best of health at present and hope to remain so. I sure do wish to be back to see my nieces and nephew and I bet they sure are pretty if they take after their mothers.
    Rosalie I am afraid I am going to stay in the Army for a few years or at least with the Government Geological Survey as I think that is the best way I can get real good at Engineering and that I consider one of the best occupations there is. All the Master Engineers that I have worked for tell me to keep at the work as they think I will make good at it.
    I will be a Corporal next month and that is doing pretty good as all the others that are Corporals are re-enlisted men and as about all the Company are old men in the service, it is pretty hard for a recruit to advance much but most of the men's time is up in five or six months and then there will be more vaccancies. I am working at present in the Company office working there in the morning and going to Surveying School in the afternoons so I do not have any drilling, Guard or K.P. and get a pass whenever I want it. If I was stationed some where in Colo. I could get a pass about every week or so and run down and see all of you folks. But when I do get back I will be able to get fourteen or 21 days leave every three months.
    Well I must close for this time. With Love, John

Ad. John G. Reuter A.P.O. 9270
Co. D 1st Engineers 2nd Brigade
A.F.I. Meisenheim, Germany

Hank was gone all summer on the harvest. Rose wondered when they would be together again. She lived for the mail and hoping word would come that they would soon be home.

La Cross, Kans.
June 23

Dear Rose,

We got here Tuesday nite at 8 oclock. The roads were a frite. The last 40 miles. Harvest wont start before Monday here. We are both working for Miller. They are nice people. There was a house burned down right here close to nite. Just about 3 hundred yds from Millers house. Don't know what started it. Just went up in smoke all at once.

I don't know what the wages will be yet. Will tell you in the next letter. Be careful about fire. love from Hank

LaCross, Kans.
June 26, 1920

Dear Rose,

This is Sunday. Clay and I are going to Sunday School with Lester Miller they talked us into the notion of going. It is only 1/2 mile to town.

Well we started to harvest Friday after noon. We will get 7 dollars a day and a long job thrashing after harvest. How are you getting along with Louie? I hope you can stick it out till I get back.

I think I can make quite a sale. I guess Clay is not going to write. The first time I wrote to you I asked him if he wanted to write some and he said no you can tell them all the news.

We had a big rain here Friday nite but didn't stop harvest. Well I guess that will be all for this time. I think I told you about the fire in the other letter. Good-bye

I am your love, Hank

La Cross, Kans.
July 1, 1920

Dear Rose,

I got your letter the other day was glad to get it to. we have been away for a week on the other place and haven't had time to write. Well my back is all write I am standing it fine. Well good bye I will write more the next time. love from Hank

LaCross, Kans.
July 6, 1920

Dear Rose,

 I got your letter Sunday and the shirts it just hapened that mine were both dirty. Well we had a big rain last nite. Clay and I were up town and had to wait till the rain was over. The rain didn't stop harvest we have worked every day except Sundays. Well we will be done harvesting in about three days.

 Say sweet hart we have decided to go north for more harvesting and not do any threshing here. They only pay 6 dollars a day and we can get 7 in the harvest and it is not so hard work. I think we will go to Colby Kans. that is about 150 miles norht west of here and come home from there. I will only have about 75 Dollars when I get done here and would like to make more if I can. I will send you some money as soon as I get paid.

 Well sweet hart I guess that is all I have to say this time. Write soon as you get this letter and then wait till I write to you for we may be gone. Good bye sweet hart. love from Hank

Colby, Kans.
July 12, 1920

R.R. 2. C.D. Pabst
Dear Rose,

 This is Sunday nite we got here this evening and got a job. The whole crew that worked for Miller at LaCross. The man we are working for has got 6 hundred acres of wheat so we will have a good long job.

 I only got $73.50 at La Cross, was going to send you some money but didn't want to put any money in the letter. I will send you some the next time I go to town.

 Say sweet hart I forgot to get them films but I will get them to you the next time I go to town. Well sweet hart it is so dark I can hardly see what I am writing so I will have to ring off. Best love from Hank

July 18, 1920

Dear Rose,

I am sending the films today this is Sunday and we don't have to work. We went to town last nite in a big Cale 8 it is sure a peach to.

Clay and I are going to Colby today to see about getting some trucks to haul wheat with. If we can get the trucks we can pay for them in about to months. They are paying 30 and 40 dollars a day for trucks and that looks good to us.

But don't say anything to any body about it for Pop will sure raise cane about us buying them. We have worked 6 days all ready and have got about two weeks yet.

I think this is the third letter I have wrote since I have been here and haven't got any yet but I know it not your fault the mail has to go so far around to get here. Well sweet hart we are ready to go to town. so good by. love from Hank R.R. 2 C.D. Pabst

Brewster, Kans.
Aug. 4, 1920

Dear Rose,

How are you getting along. We just started to thresh last evening and broke down this morning. I guess we will have to lay off the rest of the day. We are pitching bundle grain. It is not such hard work and I think I will stand it all right.

The money seems to come slow but it wont be so bad after I get in a few days. I will try to stay with it and make some money for I don't know where we will be this winter. Well sweet hart I can't think of any more to write now. Take good care of yourself.

by by sweet hart love from Hank

Brewster, Kans.
Aug. 11, 1920

Dear Rose

I got your letter and the cloths yesterday and was sure glad to hear from you it is the first I've heard from you since I've been here. I guess it has been in the office for a few days but you know I am 14 miles from town and don't get a chance to get my male or send any very often.

Well sweet hart Clay hasn't said anything about leaving Louie this time.

I am sorry you lost so many chicks. We had a big rain last nite and can't work this morning and maybe not all day. If we don't we may go to town and I can mail this to day. We have worked 3 1/2 days at $7 a day that is $24. 1/2 that is not so bad but could had that much more if we could have got a job when we first came. But we had to wait three days for a job.

I didn't sleep good last nite I guess it was because I didn't take a bath.

Well sweet hart Clay is putting gas in the old hoopey so I guess I will take a bath and put on some decent clothes and go to town.

Well by oh to my old sweet hart. loving lines from Hank
Care of Tom Johnston
P.S. I guess I didn't spell it right the other time. love from Hank Brewster, Kans.

Aug. 20. 1920

Dear Rose,

I recived your letter and the pictures the other day. The pictures were bum as you said. We had a big rain here last nite and another one this morning. I guess we wont work before Monday.

Sweet hart I was thinking awfully strong of going to Montana from here and look for a home stead. But I am on the fence and don't know which way to jump. If I was sure of getting a good place to live and work this winter I would go. But I don't know what I will do.

If the roads were not so bad I think we would have started home this morning. We were both faged out last nite. I don't know when I will be home now but it will not be long.

Maybe I can get a place here and maybe I can't but I will try. I don't think Pap wants us to have that quarter the way he talked when I told him to sell them cows and get his money back. He said he was sorry *he bought them and It would be better for me if I would get a good job. But the good job is what is bothering me.*

Well sweet hart I guess we will fair some way so don't worry. Well sweet hart I think I will see you about next week sometime but don't look for me untill you see me coming. I sure miss you a lot to sweet hart. you know it don't you. I would like to make a hundred dollars before I come home. I have only made 77 beside the 10 I let Clay have.

Well good by sweet hart. I would love to meet your lips now but I will in a few days that will seem months. Love from Hank

P.S. you didn't tell me about your lady friend.

Hank came home for a couple months and then Rose had to take the babies to stay with Janet while she was waiting for her baby to be born. Separations seemed to be the way of life on the prairie for Rose and Hank.

November 1920
Kit Carson

Dear Hank,

My dear didn't you know this is Sunday? are you sick or what is the matter. I've looked all day. did you find that piece of candy I left in the cupboard?

I started this letter last night but couldn't write anything. I lay a wake last night imagining all sort of things had happened to you. I do hope you're not sick if lf you are let me know and I'll come right home. I feel awful bad about leaving you there alone any way and I'll be home as soon as I can. The baby hasn't come yet. Say sweetheart I'm not going to take any money for staying here. They think we need it to bad and we don't do we? Me staying over here will square accounts for what I owe them.

Did you go to town Sat.? I brought your shirts and sox over here to mend and iron and I thought you would be over soon.

Say I still owe Lena 5 cents. Did you notice I took a dollar and 23 cents? Well I thought I might need it.

Say when you do come over bring some overall patches they are at the head of the bed on the floor. I didn't bring any and I couldn't mend your overalls. Are you keeping warm?

Did your sweater shrink any? Has anybody butchered since I left? Do you still love me? Did you throw that rotten meat out?

Nellie and Walt were over the other day. Mr. and Mrs. Meier were over yesterday for a few minutes. They all think Doris is it. They call her little Hank. She sure has changed since I brought her over. Well sweetheart I will close now hoping to see you or hear from you soon. Heaps of Love Your Rose

P.S. Doris says Dada and Kitty. She just loves cats. There is a little blue cat here that jumps on the bed with her. She sure is sweet. Love Rose.

Nov. 1920
Kit Carson, Colo.

Dearest Dear,

Mrs. Ramsey is over here and Dad is going to Carson tomorrow or the next day. How is your hand? and are you feeling alright? Did you throw that spoiled meat out? Did you like the pie? Do you love me? I sure am lonesome to be back with you. Do you miss me? I sure wish this was over with and Janet alright. Doris looks all over for you when I ask her "where's Hank".

I hope you are not working to hard and come over and see me before I go (crazy?) Well I will write you another letter tonight and tell you more news. Come over Sat. afternoon and stay all day Sunday won't you old top?

Doris has some shirts she sure is a good kid. I hope she doesn't forget you. Well bye bye. best love. Your Rose

P.S. will you bring over Shirley's overalls. Be sure and love Rose.

Nov. 17 1920

Dear Hank,

I received your letter and maybe I wasn't glad to hear from you. I sure was worried for a day. I imagined everything happened to you but then your letter didn't explain why you didn't come over Sunday. To tired honey? I have patched your overalls and ironed your shirts and mended some socks. I thought I would send them home with you Sunday but I didn't so I'm mailing them to you. Ira is going in tomorrow.

No sign of a baby yet they figured clear off there base from what Janet says I told her she wouldn't have it till the 24th. It seems and awful waste of time my being over here and I certainly hate to stay away from you this long. but I'm thinking I'll have to stick it out, don't you? I want to be home with you so bad. What do you fix for your breakfast and supper? Hogan's killed a beef and Ira got a hind quarter. It sure is tough.

Doris has got a tooth almost thru. She certainly is the sweet baby. She's your daughter David.

Well I've just washed my feet and teeth so I guess I will go to bed and write some more tomorrow.

Well sweetheart this is tomorrow. The baby hasn't come yet. This is sure a nice day. The kids are having a nice time. Say sweetheart would you mind going in at Hine's and ask for stork pants or rubber pants. They are about 50 cents. Doris ought to have a pair now. If you don't like to ask for them never mind. but get Shirley 2 pair black stockings size 6 1/2.

Say sweetheart Thanksgiving is a week from today and I'm planning desperatly on you coming over. Please do.

Do you feed your cat? and chickens? are they growing?

Well sweetheart I'm closing for this time. write soon.

Best love from Rose

P.S. Mrs. Hogan was over yesterday. I just put a little fudge in the box. I'll make you lots when I come home.

Rose Eads
Nov. 17, 1920

Dear Rose,

I wish to christ you would come home. I am sure getting sick of staying alone. Is the baby born yet? I sure hope it is so you can come home. I have to work from the time I get up in the morning till I go to bed at nite getting breakfast and supper. Well sweet hart I didn't get to come up there Sunday I thought of coming but I dreaded the ride so. I got a load of coal Saturday and picked cow chips Sunday.

Paul and Raymond were here Saturday nite and stayed all nite. Raymond helped me pick cow chips Sunday.

Pap is getting worse all the time. Hopkins comes out every other day and gives him morphene he says it stops the pane and makes him sleep.

Say sweet hart what did you do with my brown pants? I have upset every thing in the house and haven't found them yet. I am about out of clothes. Betsy patched a pare for me tonite with overall patches.

Well sweet hart why don't you write. I haven't heard from you yet. This is only the second one I have wrote but I haven't had a chance to mail any. I am thinking and hope you will be home before you get this letter but I will write any how.

Ma said maybe Rose has left you. I said I guess she has for a while any way. Well good nite sweet. I have to get up at 4 in the morning now. from Hank

In November, the doctor was sent for and Dora Jean was born. Rose was staying with Janet until the baby came, and the Ramsey's, Meier's and McGinty's dropped in to bring food. Janet and Ira didn't have a very big house. It was only two rooms, but it was made of stone. Somehow they all managed to fit.

Another winter on the prairie, in the soddy and no hope of life getting any better. When there was no snow the wind blew, but at least it was easier to get to town or to a neighbor to talk to once in a while. When it was possible, the women would get together for a quilting bee. The children could play outside, and the women could chat and sew all afternoon.

Hank was changing jobs. He wasn't needed on the Thompson ranch for the winter, so he had a job in Kansas driving cattle to another state. He would be gone for weeks at a time.

Rose did not take this news lightly. She let Hank know exactly how she felt about being left on the prairie all alone with the babies. It was bad enough that he had his tobacco and boots when there was hardly any food in the house. Rose had nagged on about

Hank having to have his tobacco and boots, even when there was no money, ever since he returned from the war. She was always reminding him that she didn't spend any of his money while he was in the war. She went without things she needed so he would have money when he returned. Hank would never say anything when she was in this mood.

Hank left for Kansas and said he would write when he could get to a post office, and he would send her money every time he got paid. He wouldn't need much as he got meals when he was driving the cattle.

Rose would gather cow chips to burn to keep the soddy warm and covered the window to keep the blowing dust out.

Ira came to get her and the babies from time to time so she could be with her sister Janet.

Rose was so happy to be with her sister. Janet always had people dropping in. Mrs. Ramsey was a frequent visitor along with Mrs. Meier and her daughter Irma.

Mrs. Ramsey told the story about her husband Walter and another man who were in a camp on the prairie when some Indians on the warpath came upon their camp and entered the tent. Walter was the first they approached, and they pulled off his hat. He was bald. The Indians were superstitious, and they thought he had already been scalped, so they fled.

When Ira would visit the Ramseys, Mrs. Ramsey would always give him vegetables and cucumbers, but on his way home he threw the cucumbers away. When she would visit soon after, she saw the cucumbers along the road. She asked Ira why he threw away the cucumbers? He told her they considered them poisonous.

While Rose was staying with Janet, they got a lot of canning done. This would last them through the winter and spring.

Hank came home for Thanksgiving, and they went to the Kirby's in Eads for dinner. They had missed several Sundays already.

Rose nagged Hank about living so far away from everyone, she didn't like being stuck on the prairie all alone with the children. He said there was nothing he could do about it, but maybe they could live on the Lyle place, he thought it was empty.

After Christmas, they moved to the Lyle place, and Hank had to return to Kansas for a while.

Janet and Ira moved also, into a two-room rock house. Ira was starting his herd of polled Herefords. Ranching was his chosen vocation.

The house stood barren on the prairie, not a tree in sight. The ground around the house was blown clean by the wind. The windmill out by the stock tank stood like a sentinel. All was quiet except the creaking of the windmill blades as the wind danced through them.

Toys for the children were empty wooden spools for thread. Johnny had an old truck and Shirley had a doll, but she spent most of her time taking care of Doris, so Rose could wash and iron and cook.

Hank arrived in March just in time for plowing under last year's crop. Then the ground had to be harrowed before planting new crops. Rose planted a vegetable garden so they would have plenty to can in the fall.

Rose and Janet wrote to their brother John as often as they could, but didn't get a reply very often. They thought about Ruth and wondered what kind of life she had.

Rose wanted some chickens so they could have eggs, even though Janet and Ira had plenty to share. They would get together and take the children out on the prairie to gather lamb's quarters. It was an edible green plant something like collard greens.

One of the ranchers had a milk cow, and she and Janet would take the buckboard to get milk. They were still nursing Doris and Dora Jean, but Johnny and Shirley needed milk. Ira said he would get Janet a milk cow so they could have plenty of heavy cream and the milk for cooking.

Sometimes Ira and Hank would ride as a cowboy into the night and bring a dollar home as their pay. Coyote hides brought a good price, so Ira had skinned and cured about thirteen hundred dollars worth of hides. A traveling buyer bought them with a bad check. Christmas that year was lean as were others that followed. Uncle John Reuter showed up to play Santa Claus.

They all got together at Janet and Ira's. It was so good to see their brother and catch up on all his news. He was amazed at the children, his nieces and nephew. This was the first time he had met Ira or Hank.

He was still looking for brother Joe. Last he heard, he was in Kansas, but he didn't know where. They figured Ruth must be sixteen now. John was twenty one and not married yet. He had a good job in Missouri at a grocery store. He hoped to start his own store, but times were bad, so he would wait.

September rolled around and Rose gave birth to a baby boy they named Donald. Doris was still in diapers and nursing. It was time for Doris to give up the crib and sleep with Shirley. It wasn't much of a crib, more of a cradle made of pine. Mrs. Ramsey was always good about rounding up items for the babies. She was always helping someone and a midwife besides.

Shirley was five now and a big help, taking care of the babies.

Rose washed their clothes and diapers on the scrub board after heating the water over a fire. Water was hauled from the creek. A line was strung between two posts and had to be supported in the middle with a long stick. Soap was made with the lard when a pig was butchered.

Janet and Ira killed a pig, dipped the hog into the barrel of hot water, scraped the skin and hung the carcass on the windmill tower for butchering. Then came the chore of preserving every inch of the pig.

Rose kept in touch with the Palmer family in Denver and would write to them four or five times a year, telling them how much Shirley had grown. Then one day she received a letter from Mother Palmer informing her that her husband, the Judge, had died. He had a severe heart attack and the doctor couldn't save him. Rose took the news very hard. It seemed like all the people who were good to her were all dying. This didn't make her life on the prairie any easier.

Living at the Lyle Place was not so far from other neighbors, but Rose still wasn't very happy about her lot in life. When Hank was home she nagged him to do something and when he did she nagged him because that wasn't what she wanted done. He could plow the field and she would walk along side of him carrying the baby on her hip nagging all the while.

Hank had only gone to the fourth grade when he took off for Montana at the age of fourteen. He could write and do numbers, but he hadn't read any books. Winters, when they were confined to the house, Rose would read to him out loud. When she wasn't yelling or screaming at him.

There were about one hundred residents of Kit Carson in the 1920's and everyone knew everyone. The get-togethers were lively. There was dancing and food in the big hall in town. The Meiers owned the grocery store. There was a lumber yard, a barber shop, the Evans Hotel, a restaurant, hardware store, the post office and the bank on Main Street.

There was a new brick school house going up in town. The territory was so vast that there were little school houses all over the county so the children wouldn't have to go so far from home. Many had only six or seven students of all ages. Many times the children in the upper grades would board with families that lived in town. That way they could attend the new school and finish the eighth grade. It was a special event to attend the eighth grade graduation. None of the farmers had a lot of money, but the girls had the prettiest dresses. Their mothers would order material from a catalog, and they would make the dresses. They even made the boys' suits for the occasion.

Many children had September birthdays due to their parents being snowed in during the hard winters. So it was evident that Janet would give birth to her third child in September. The baby weighed only four pounds, and the doctor set her aside to care for Janet. He said the baby wouldn't live. Mrs. Ramsey started working on the baby, and she responded with a loud cry. They named her Lydia Martella.

Shirley would soon be six and she was eager to start school. Pleasant Valley school was two miles from the Lyle place. Just a one room frame house with no trees around; just flat barren land. There was an out house behind, next to the woodpile. In the front were hitching posts for those who rode a horse to school. The teacher would live with one of the families of her students.

One of Shirley's playmates lived on the other side of Rush Creek, and he too would go to Little Victor School.

Rose had her hands full with Doris and Donald, who were two and one years old. She would miss Shirley's help while she was in school.

Wash day was hard. First you had to build a good hot fire and set the boiler on the stove and haul the water from the windmill. Scrub the clothes on a washboard, have a second tub full of rinse water. Every item of clothing had to be rung by hand first in the soapy water and second in the rinse water. The clothes were made of heavy cotton and denim. Sheets were rough muslin. Pillow cases and underwear were made from flour sacks. Some were flowery and some were plain.

After washing and hanging everything on the clothesline, *everything* had to be ironed. When the women had some idle time they embroidered pillow cases and table cloths.

CHAPTER 7

HOMESTEAD LIFE 1922

What a treat to get some mail. Rose got a letter from Grandma Gillis in Sedro Wooley. She was doing poorly, she was suffering from Erysipelas, but Aunt Rosalie was a big help to her. She would love to see the children, if it were at all possible. Rose was in no position to travel to Washington and neither was Grandma able to travel to Colorado.

Hank was in Brewster, Kansas, on a cattle drive. He had word from his father that he had better come back and take care of the cattle he was taking care of for him. He was pretty disgusted and wished he had never gotten involved with him.

Hank was ready to take off for Montana and see if there were any homestead possibilities there and then he would send for Rose and the children. He was not coming home until he had made a hundred dollars, he had seventy-seven now after he loaned nine dollars to his brother Clay.

Rose wrote back to him and told him to come home to her as soon as possible. They would work it out somehow. She was not overjoyed with the prospect of moving back to the homestead. Living in the soddy was not her idea of living.

The homestead was in Lamar, which is halfway between Eads and Kit Carson, not close to either family, but now that Hank was back they went to his family every Sunday for dinner. They were not surprised that Rose was in the family way again.

One Sunday, as Hank and Rose arrived for dinner at Virgil and Carrie Kirby's house, there was so much commotion and crying, they couldn't figure out what happened. Then Hank's brother Dallas told him that "Pap" had shot himself with a 410 shotgun. Dallas was beating the gun against a tree shattering it to smithereens.

"Pap" had an operation four years before for bladder and prostate cancer. He wore a bag and had a urine tube for drainage. He couldn't take it any more and waited until the whole family was at his house and did away with himself.

Not long after "Pap" died, Hank received another letter from the Department of the Interior, United States Land Office, stating that he had insufficient residence on the land. He was twenty three days short. He had thirty days to cure the defects or appeal this decision to the Commissioner of the General Land Office.

When Hank returned from Kansas, they moved back to the soddy and Hank started writing to the government telling them his absence began on September 28th, 1922. He was allowed to be absent no more than five months. This was the beginning of many letters.

Hank was beside himself, trying to support his family and work the land and very little money coming in. He barely had enough money to buy seed. Maybe he could make a little when he harvested his crop in the Fall.

He received a letter from the government asking if Hank was living on the homestead. He was to let them know how many days he lived on the land each year. If he didn't have enough days, he would lose the land.

Everyone was getting gasoline automobiles, and Hank was able to get a Maxwell from one of the neighbors that wanted a new Ford. This made the trips to visit a little more comfortable.

Rose gave birth to Daniel Lloyd on March 15, 1923. The soddy was getting crowded. Shirley was almost like a mother to Donald and Doris now that the new baby had arrived. Three babies under three years old. The youngest child was always called baby until the next one arrived. When Janet and Rose got together they had quite a housefull of kids. It seemed like they were taking turns having kids.

Mrs. P.L. Palmer
1250 Ogden Street
Denver, Colo.

March 23, 1923
My Dear Rose,
    I have kept your letter and each week thought I would write you I even carried it with me to California where I have been for the last two months and a half. Just came home last Sunday not having written you as I intended.
    There has been so much for me to attend to with the business and my work that each day has been so full of the things that needed to be attended to.
    Well Rose you perhaps most of any one except Clare knows what mly life is without my dear husband and since we were alone we had come to be like one soul that it seems one half of me is gone. He was just sick one week from the day he was brought home from the office in great pain across his lungs and heart. But the Drs. had given us great incourgement and he seemed to be getting better and overdid and the heart gave out among his dear dear ones over there together and we two here. Is life not a strange thing?
    Clare and Gladys came to live here with me. You know I had made the uptairs into an apt I rent it for $95 a month. Made a kitchenette out of the china closet downstairs and a bathroom of the back pantry and a bedroom of the the old kitchen. We use the back parlor for diningroom and the old livingroom for a bedroom. C & G have that for theirs but life is so changed I I have not yet made my permanent plans it is so hard to know just the very best thing to do for all concerned. The children have been dear and kind but of course it is hard to plan for two families.
    Clifford is well but not married. We hear from him quite often and it always seems good to hear. But of course his life is young and he will probably marry again and I hope he will not. Never will he find one

like my precious girl I am afraid. Oh, she was so dea and how I have to turn to God and Christ when I look back. As you said in your letter, only God and Christ know best. My faith and religion helps me and I go on doing my work and making life as bright as I can.

I am so interested in your little family and hope you kept the veil that was over his face. You know he might be a Charles Dickens, he was born with one and it was sold for many pounds.

How we would love to see little Jannet. Holcomb remembers her and we often talk of those days. He is doing well in the first grade in school.

Gladys and her mother have gone to Mrs. Slatterys for luncheon. That sounds natural I know.

Dorothy across the road still sits on the porch and does not seem to have any beau. We cannot understand, she is much older looking and always with her mother.

Ewald is quite a man and they are building a garage next to our property.

Did you know that Mrs. Gaylord died last summer and Ellen has a new home in Country Club Place.

Rose I think I have told you all the news and must write some other letters. You know Rose I always feel so near to you different to any one else. I helped you through your experience and you were so dear to my darling Alice that I will always feel you a part of our life and will be so interested in all you are doing and in our little Jannet. Do you never come to Denver? You must come to see us if you do.

I forgot to tell you after Mr. Bullen died Mrs. Bullen closed the house and she and Adeline went to Europe and are now in Egypt. They wanted me to come to them when father died but I could not bear to go away from here.

Always with love , Mrs. Palmer

However, most of the families on the prairie had nine or ten kids usually each one two years apart.

The County was getting ready to build new bridges that had been washed out during the last floods. Hank went to see if he could get on the construction crew.

About the time Hank was starting on the bridges, he received a certificate of consummation of land signed by the President Calvin Coolidge. He could stay on the Homestead.

Hank was building bridges on Rush Creek, Sand Creek and a washout at Chivington as long as the weather was good, but when the snow fell and the blizzards blew they were holed up in their soddy.

Ira and Janet moved into the Lyle Place. Ira needed to move his cattle to better pasture. The house wasn't much bigger, but there were a few trees around it.

Rose and Hank's baby was just a little over a year when Janet gave birth to another girl. They named her Mary Alice.

Once Hank received full ownership of his land by living on it and making improvements over a certain amount of time, he could then move closer to town. He went to work for a farmer named Long, house included. Hank was back driving cattle and plowing the fields.

Hank was gone for days at a time, riding the range. Rose had the car to go visit her sister, and sometimes she went to Eads to see Hank's sisters.

Shirley and Doris were both in school now, and sometimes Rose would drive them to school along with their neighbors' children. Don rode along and the baby rode on Rose's lap. There wasn't anyone to leave the younger children with, so they all had to go along.

Grandma Kirby made the statement that all seven of her grandchildren were here all together, but when Doris counted she came up with one more than Grandma, and she said, "No sir, Grandma, there are eight."

Grandma said," Shirley is not of my blood. There are only seven."

Shirley was so confused. What did she mean, *not of her blood?* How would Rose tell Shirley the truth?

The homestead had a watering tank next to the windmill and the kids liked to play in the water. One day Don was hanging over the edge of the tank when he fell in and couldn't swim, Doris went running to the house to get help. Luckily Hank was close, and he ran to the tank and fished Don out choking and half drowned.

Hank was struggling to make a go of the homestead, planting and plowing. He still helped the other farmers round up cows and calves for branding. He would be gone for days at a time. His brother Martin needed help with his spread now that their father was gone.

His brother Martin had just gotten married, and they took the house three miles south of their parents' place so their mother could depend on them when she needed something.

Rose now was expecting her fifth child, so she spent as much time as possible with her sister Janet. They would take the buckboard over to the neighbors with canned pickles and other vegetables from their garden and bring back whatever their neighbors had in excess. Sometimes it would be a rocking chair or a baby bed.

While Rose was visiting Janet, Ira brought the mail in from town and there were two letters, one from their Aunt Rosalie in Sedro Wooley, Washington, and one from their long lost brother, Joseph. They read Aunt Rosalie's letter first. It started out apologizing for not sending Rose her own letter. The news was not good, as she wished to inform them of their Grandmother Gillis's death. She went on to say that she had been failing for the last year, and it is a blessing she doesn't have to suffer any longer. She will be buried next to their momma.

Janet and Rose thought about all that had happened since that day sixteen years ago. They were anxious to see what news their brother had.

Third Engineers
Schofield Barracks, Hawaii
August 24, 1925

Dearest Sisters,
Well, kids, I have at last started on the upward road of Army life.

I have just been in my company two months and I was made first class private the other day, which pays nine more dollars a month. Oh! I do hate this Army life, but even so I have to make the most of it. I have collected three hundred pictures already and I expect to get several more before I leave here.

Gee! I am sorry that John doesn't get married. I am afraid he is getting too much of the wanderlust in his veins, but even so I don't see what there is in life anyway, except just live and die and that is the same as every animal does. Say I do doubt there being a hereafter, what do we do that we should deserve any eternal bliss, as is promised in the bible.

My Captain likes me fine, but that is very little consolation, life is just one up and down and then back to dust for us. I don't get any kick out of it any more, and I guess that I will return home and get married and ease my way on through the few remaining years.

I'll send you an Army photo of myself one of these days. I am getting rather big now. I weigh about one hundred eighty pounds, and I'm not fat either.

How is each of the kids now? I bet Shirley is looking forward to school again. Rather wish I was back in school myself. I love to study philosophy and history and math. I was the damndest fool for ever trying to study religion, it sickened me of school temporarily, and I enlisted right then.

How are the crops there? Things grow here always.

Well, sis's I can't think of any more to write, right now, so I'll write again soon.

Lovingly, Joseph

Rose and Janet were so moved by their brother's letter, they had to sit quietly for a few minutes and wonder over all that he had said. They wiped their tears and both said silently that they would have to get a letter off to him as soon as supper was over.

Less than a month later, Rose got a return letter from their brother, Joseph. she could hardly wait to read it to Janet.

The Hawaiian Division

Schofield Barracks, Hawaii
September 5, 1925

Dear Sister,

    Received a letter from you this eve and I was glad as could be. You state that Shirley doesn't know the difference. Why in heck didn't you tell me before? I didn't know what you were calling her. She will be started to school again by the time you receive this letter, and I hope she enjoys it better than she most likely will, for few kids care much for school.

    Well, sis, I am sending you a picture in this and I am also sending you a folder by way of Janette, I am sending one to John too, just sent them together.

    I am having quite a time at present, keeping up with the rest of the world, for this is a dull place to be. I am going out to target practice about the fifteenth, I am a fair shot.

    Say, I wont cry a bit when I get out of this Army. I guess I'll buy out about next May. I am not certain yet what I will do. It all depends on my girl, and whether anything else of importance happens.

    It seems queer to have you speak of frost. This is one place where snow never did show its face and it is very monotonously the same here all the time. I am pretty well acclimated now, but gee, I am tender, why I can hardly rub my hands together without wearing blisters on them.

    I had a row with the mess Sergeant today and I am pretty apt to get his place if he doesn't watch his step. For I have enough evidence on him to put him in Army prison for three to eight years. He thinks he is too smart, and I'll teach him to handle me with gloves on, for I am quite hot-headed myself, in fact, I have sent four men to the hospital since I arrived over here, and I do not object to sending a few more. Tell Hank that the army is hell itself. I guess he knows it.

    Well, I must close, with love, Joseph

Rose and Janet looked at the pictures and wondered if their brother would make it out of the Army alive. They didn't realize he had such a temper. They couldn't remember him as a child, being angry. He was quiet and maybe he was storing up all his anger for later.

Rose and Janet were kept busy with the babies and canning, the cucumbers were abundant and they pickled them by the bushels. The little ones and the deformed ones were called gerkins. Never would you find such a delicious treat, each spice enhanced the flavor.

Life on the prairie was not a picnic, but the way they made the best of what they had, helped to make it bearable. The cellar was packed with enough food to last the winter when the blizzards came and isolated them for days. There was always concern for the poor animals and provisions had to be made for them.

What a relief when the winds died down and little patches of green were showing up and the crocus were blooming. Then the dogs days of summer set in.

Rose and Janet were so surprised when they had a letter from their sister Ruth. The address was from Mrs. Edward Wells Stowe in Glenview, Illinios. She had just turned twenty one and her adoptive family helped her find her sisters and brothers.

Ruth goes on to tell them she married Edward in 1922. He was nineteen when his family adopted her and he said he would wait until she was of age and he would marry her.

Ruth had just given birth to her third child, Edward Wells Jr. Their first child Bertha Wells was now three and Winifred Louise was almost two.

She was so happy to find her family and let them know that she was ok and now they can get reaquainted. She wanted them to write often and tell her all about their families Rose and Janet made it a point to write to her. They were so glad to hear from her, now they have all been accounted for.

The summer was busy and everyone did as much visiting as they could to prepare for the long lonely winter. The harvest was just about over and the first snowfall wasn't far off. Just before Thanksgiving Rose went into labor and gave birth to another boy. They named him Henry Verner Kirby, Jr., after his dad.

Shirley was now ten years old, and she was looking after her younger brothers and sister like they were her own. She took charge of the new baby while Rose was recuperating from his birth. Each birth seemed to weaken her more, and she was very run down and thin.

The children spent a lot of time with their cousins; they were all close to the same age. Shirley, Johnny, Dora Jean and Doris were all in school, and their teacher was Olive Woodward. She became close to the two families and stayed with Janet and Ira through the winter months.

It had been awhile since they had heard from their brother Joseph, so they were surprised and delighted to get a letter from him. The postmark was Shreveport, Louisiana. It was not an Army post, so he must have gotten out of the Army in one piece.

January 26, 1927

Dearest Sis:

Got your letter yesterday, and was so glad to hear from you. Of course I am going to write to Shirley, she no doubt received my letter to her by now. I am enclosing another dollar for her for this week and will not write to her again until she writes to me, however I will endeavor to send her the dollar each week either to you or to her direct, I want you to encourage her to save, for that has been my policy for several years, and I am not of any other mind but that it is a wonderful policy, for it at least gives one the feeling of security, having money in the bank.

Ruth seemingly has forgotten me as swiftly as she found me, as I have not received but one letter from her in all. I am surprised as hell as slightly hurt, perhaps though there is some reason for the delay.

The climate here is far too wonderful to describe, and I would be very foolish indeed to move to other parts. This town I am quite sure shall always be my home, unless of course the unforeseen should decree otherwise.

I am glad that John has been able to go see Ruth. Just how well is John getting along, I mean in the ways of the world? You see he never writes to me any more, although I am as much interested in him now as I ever was, and that is really a whole lot.

  Jeanette has not written for a week or so but she does write real often.

  I am now earning sixty dollars a week and never did I imagine that I would receive money that easy, but I guess there is something in my manner that appeals to people, at least that is what my two bosses say, and so they raised me another ten dollars a week. I am showing my appreciation by doing the best work I know how, but the best I can do is keep busy three hours a day and the rest of the time I sit here and write letters to you and others that are close to me. It is really a snap.

  Did I tell you that I purchased a new Chevrolet? It is the bunk, and next fall I plan to trade it in on a Buick or Chrysler or some such car as that.

  I am sending some stamps for Shirley, for I know that you are a long ways from town, have her write often, for it is good practice if nothing more. Write when you get time.

Most Lovingly,
Joseph.

  Rose wondered if Joseph realized how long it had been since he had written. She remembered when he was so desperate that he tried to get Ruth's share of the inheritance, which wasn't much, but the trustee wouldn't release it to him because they had located Ruth and she was very much alive. However, she wouldn't get her inheritance until she turned twenty one.

  Reference was made to the subject of the children's inheritance while they were still in the State Home, but it seemed that only Ruth was to inherit whatever Clem had not absconded with or drank up. Who the trustee was is a mystery. Was it the State of Colorado?

  When Ruth got her inheritance, which was only about two or three hundred dollars, she bought a desk. (Her son, Edward Wells Jr., has that desk as of this day.)

CHAPTER 8

DENVER 1927

It was June, now, 1927 and Miss Woodward was going to visit her family for the summer. Janet would miss her, especially since she had just given birth to her fifth child. He was named Ira Everett McKeever, Jr.

There was an epidemic of Infantile Paralysis going around and when Danny got sick, the doctor treated him as best he could and told Rose he would have to go to Denver to Children's Hospital for treatment. He could get worse if he didn't.

Hank was working in Eads, and she had to send word to him that she had to take Danny to Denver. She left Doris and Don with Janet and Ira. Shirley went along, she was eleven now, and she took the baby too, he was still nursing.

Rose went straight to Mother Palmer's when she got to Denver and told her she had to put Danny in the hospital that day. Mother Palmer said she was welcome to stay with her when she wasn't visiting Danny.

Hospital visiting hours were very strict, Rose could only see Danny for a half hour, mid-morning and afternoon.

The doctors told Rose that Danny would have to be hospitalized for several weeks and quarantined, as his disease was contagious.

Rose wrote to Hank and told him she would have to stay in Denver for quite some time, and for him to check on the kids every chance he could get.

1210 Clarkson
Sunday

Dear Hank,

I'm feeling more relieved tonight. I have been over to the hospital and Hank, there never was a more patient child than Dan. His mouth turned in to se me and he cried from gladness, but we got along famously, but it just tears my heart out to leave him. Mrs. Palmer is expecting me to leave for down there some time this week. She says for me to go back down there and get my affairs straightened out then we can look for a place and move closer to Denver where we can be closer to Dan. Dr. Packer has not made up his mind yet about Dan, what his treatment will be or how bad he is damaged. what all are you doing? what do you think we ought to do? Lots of love, Rose

August 29

Dear Rose,

I got your letter today. I sure don't know what to do or think. I was sure there was something there I could do. You can't come back and leave Dan there. It must be awful for him to not have you with him. Why wont they let you be with him more. What kind of a Dr. is he and what kind of treatments are they giving him. I didn't go to see the kids Sunday. I went to get Walter, but he and another kid was going to town. Morgan would have taken me, but I hated to ask him. Vera was here Friday and didn't find any one. I got in from the field about dark and she was just leaving, I talked to her about five minutes on the road, Ethel wasn't feeling well and stayed in town. They want you to write to them. How did you stand the change? Is Shirley and the baby well? Morgan thinks I am foolish to stay here. By from Hank

1210 Clarkson St.
Denver, Colo.
Aug. 29, 1927

Dear Hank,

I will be over at the hospital again tomorrow to see Dan. I was over Sunday and he was the bravest little tike. He wants to so hard to get better and come home. He says that if Hank would come and stay with him that I could go anywhere I wanted to, but it is against all rules to stay longer than half an hour on visiting days.

Mr. Palmer and I investigated a prospect of a job today, but they didn't want a man they wanted a slave for $60.00 a month and I had to do as much as you did. Mr. Palmer said he felt sure there was better jobs than that if we didn't rush too fast. I wish you could have seen the house they wanted us to live in.

Mrs. Benidict is coming home tomorrow and Palmers are going to see what she has to offer.

Mrs. Palmer said that the thing to do would be for me to go back down home and they would watch out for a job for you.

Hank it is so hard write I don't know exactly what to tell you. What is Kern doing? Did you get to see the kids Sunday? Well I am waiting to hear from you. How did you get home Friday?

We are getting several nurses and head people over at the hospital interested in Dan so that he will feel he is not alone over there. The nurses say he is the best little fellow.

We sent Mrs. Palmer a night letter to let her know where Dan is and what he is doing and that we wanted to locate near Denver so if there are any ropes to be pulled she will pull them.

I do so hope that there will be something soon and to our advantage.

I'm sending the visiting card. It is sure strict. Well I must go to bed. Write soon. Best of love. From Rose

By the time Hank came in from the range and rode into town to get the mail and fixed some beans and fried potatoes, he fell into bed too tired to ride over to Ira's to see the kids.

The longer Rose stayed in Denver the worse it got for Hank to stay in Eads without her and the kids.

Denver, Colo.
Sept. 1, 1927

Dearest Hank,
You know no matter how I feel about not being with Dan is noth-

ing if it will make him learn to raise himself and get around straight. The reason he must be in the hospital Dr. Packard is 2nd in the U.S. in that line and he has done very wonderful work.

Miss Fackt has charge of the muscle training and she is head of her line so we are very lucky Hank to have these friends here take an interest as you know there wont be a stone left unturned to bring back as much as can be brought back and I feel Hank that no sacrifice is too great to make Dan better.

He wants to come home every time he sees me but is a little angel about not whimpering. It just tears my heart out to leave him but I don't dare let him know.

Don't think about my doing any work Hank, it can't be done. Dr. said I had to wean Vern for his sake and mine. I will have 3 kids for school and getting over to the hospital three times a week. Well, I think I will be kept pretty busy.

Palmer's are watching out all the time for a job for you. Just anything within reason to do till a better one turns up. Rent is terrible.

What do you think of taking everything of ours up to Janet's and having her send what we need when we need it. She can pack the dishes in the bed clothes and that would be about the first things we would need. Don't move that old cabinet or table again and the beds aren't worth moving. The chairs are not worth bringing up here.

You know there are a lot of second hand stores here. That stove isn't worth taking off the place. But be sure and take the curtains and blinds down. If Janet wants the blinds let her have them. Get all the clothes and letters and pictures, sell the chickens.

Say Hank we are stacked knee deep here. What do you suppose about getting your ticket to Littleton and looking there for work.

You couldn't make enough working by the day to keep up the rent and eats and maybe there is work where people want people to live on their places for shares with everything furnished. I sure want you to get near Denver for I must see Dan when I am allowed.

Mr. P is watching out for a job all the time and we will let you know right away. But don't bring the household stuff up without a place to put it, it isn't worth bringing up anyway.

I wish we had a place too, for I'm afraid we are wearing our welcome out.

Vern isn't well he has a cold and don't feel a bit good. And Mrs. P is working all the time. She is nice, but I want to live in my own.

Mr. P. don't approve of you coming to Denver and leaving that job, and on the other hand he says no one will hire a man thru the wife.

Mrs. Brown has a family on their place has had them for years. Do you suppose Doris and Don will be alright at Janets till you are settled somewhere?

I don't know what to do or say. What do you think? Well good night.

Palmer's are out tonight, maybe they will hear of something. I'll write a little in the morning. Tomorrow is my day to see Dan. Oh, I'm heartsick about that tike.

We don't notice any difference in the change. Dr. said both Dan's legs were good, well night. Sleep tight.

How are you making out? Send Dodd's address please I'm going to write to them.

Well this is morning and nothing new. If you think there is anything at Loveland or Longmont try it. I want to get all together too in a place where I can come back and forth and see Dan. And where there is pretty good living condition. Keep me posted where you are.

We can leave Don and Doris at Janet's till you find something. See if they are well. Bye Love, Rose

Lamar
Friday
September 2, 1928

Dear Rose,

I got your letter today. No I haven't seen the kids yet. I wanted to go up there today, but Walter was working. I have irrigated three nights. Morgan told Albert I was leaving, so I guess I will. I think I will start for Denver Monday or Tuesday. I will see the kids first. I don't know what to do with the household. It is so far to haul it up to Janettes. I think I will take the sewing machine and dishes and leave the rest here, unless you find something by Monday.

Are Palmer's getting tired of you being there? How is your money holding out? You will have to brace up and don't get sick. Tell Dannie I will see him in a few days.

I thought I might get a job in some warehouse or freight depot. Morgan said his brother-in-law is making four to five dollars a day at the stock yards. I think if I was there and pick a few jobs and just lay for them there, maybe a vacancy in a day or two.

Louis is at Loveland, he says there is plenty of work there. He is making four dollars a day and board.

I was thinking if you could get a couple of rooms, I would bring the kids and household, and maybe you could get some sewing to do and I could do anything I could get. There will surely be work in the country around there. Threshing is probably on now.

Virgil Lite makes a trip to Denver twice a week, with a five ton truck. Morgan says I can get him to take us and the household, up there for about what it would cost me to go on the train. Have you said anything about the Mrs. Brown farm yet or the stock yards?

Think this over and let me know before Saturday. I would like to get us all together as soon as possible. I don't want you to go away and leave Dan. I will try to see the kids some evening. I didn't get home from town until three o'clock Friday. Bye, Hank

Rose did not take this news lightly, she was furious with Hank for suggesting such an idea. She wrote back immediately and told him just to leave things the way they were. She can't take care of the baby and sew and still see Danny. It is so hard to leave him, and he looks so sad when she has to go.

Soon Hank arrived with the sewing machine and all the kids in tow. They found a house on Twenty Second and Franklin. The next day Hank went looking for a job.

Donald was old enough now to start school with his sisters, so they were enrolled in Whittier School at Twenty fourth and Marion. Rose had only the baby at home during the day. She would leave Shirley in charge, after school, when she visited Danny.

Hank couldn't find work in Longmont, so he went south to

Larkspur. Mr. Long had some other property around Castle Rock and he needed a foreman. He could get to Denver easier than from Eads. He lived in the bunkhouse.

Somehow the mail caught up with Rose and Hank in all their moves, and of all things they got a letter from her brother Joseph. The postmark was from Elizabeth, Colorado.

April 25, 1928
Elizabeth, Colo.

Dear Rosalie,

I suppose Jannette has already told you that I have moved back to my old home. I have been back for a little more than a month now. I am just beginning to feel well again. I have been sick for five or six months.

It surely is queer what troubles one will have for such a short life as we have here on this old world. Really at times I feel that I would have much rather my parents would have never seen fit to have brought me into this cruel world, which I find so full of avarice and selfishness and continual strive, not so much with the elements as with one another.

I am of the opinion that I will never marry, for truly I would feel that I was doing an awful thing to bring into this world others to have them suffer the trials and tribulations that I have already gone through and I feel that my troubles are very minor in comparison to yours.

Lovingly, Joseph

Danny was showing some improvement and Rose was given a list of exercises for Danny to do to strengthen his muscles. He was allowed to go home for a few hours on weekends. When school was out they went to live in Larkspur where Hank was given a house.

It looked like Danny would be all right, even though he had to wear a back brace and leg braces when he was not in bed. He made it through the winter without getting sick, but the doctor said he should have his tonsils out before another winter.

Danny played with his brother Don when school was out for the summer. He was improving and could run with his braces.

After the children went back to school, it was decided that Danny should have his tonsils out. November, he went to the hospital and while recuperating from the surgery there was a flu epidemic. In his weakened condition he came down with the flu. It would be weeks before he could go home.

Rose drove to the hospital every day to see him, but on one of her trips she had the baby with her and just as she approached the railroad tracks, she saw a train, she gave the steering wheel a hard pull to the right to miss the train and went over an embankment. When help came to her rescue, they found she had a broken leg and numerous cuts. The baby had a severe head injury that looked like a spike in his head. They were rushed to the hospital in Denver.

Hank took the kids to the Kaestners, some friends of theirs in North Denver. He couldn't take care of them and work too.

December 9, 1928

Dear Rose,

I got your note today. It is sure too bad if your arm is paralyzed. I hope it don't last long. I got two loads of wood today thinking you would be home by the middle of the week. I haven't seen the kids since Wednesday and can't get in before next Wednesday. Mr. Long is sick in Denver, he hasn't been out all week. We are pretty busy here. We are going to butcher a beef on Tuesday or Wednesday. I will take a chunk in to Kaestners.

Are you out of quarantine yet? Did you get your shoes? I hope they are satisfactory. Have you walked yet? I will bring you candy and apples when I come, but I haven't any money for paper and envelopes.

Poor Dan will think we have left him for good this time. They wouldn't let me see him the last time I was in. They have him in a big room with other kids now so it won't be so hard on him. Will try to see you Wednesday. Bye from Hank

The Kaestners were good friends of Rose and Hank and all the kids were staying with them in North Denver, on Thirty Eighth and Hooker. It was not close to the hospital, which was on Nineteenth and Gilpin.

Danny was in one hospital and his mother and little brother were in a different one. Danny couldn't figure out why no one came to see him. He was only five and wasn't told about the accident. A few days later Hank was seriously ill and had to go to the hospital.

Hank was in the men's ward and Rose was in the women's ward. The only way they could communicate was by writing letters to each other.

Rose would write to Hank in the men's ward, she had a hard time writing with her arm in a cast.

Dear Hank,
    I didn't go out just because I couldn't, when you felt the way you do and besides Dr. Gaede said if I didn't have to work it would be alright, but I'm apt to work. Mr. Long don't think I had better. If you run a normal temperature Saturday I may go home and see what I can do. Now, Mind me and keep your shoulders covered. I'll try and see you in the morning. The funeral is at one thirty, they will come and get me around noon. You do care about me don't you? You do know you help me, the main thing now is for you to get well and come home and take up the reins again.
    Dear Hank, I dread going home again. I had forgot how the children looked. I'm sending you a little pencil to you if you want to do any writing.

Love, Rose

Hank's brother Martin and his wife, Evie, drove up from Eads to see them and couldn't get in. They had to write a note from the desk in the lobby to ask if they could visit the patients.

There was an influenza epidemic going around and in Danny's weakened condition, he succumbed and died. It was December Seventeenth, Nineteen Hundred and Twenty Eight. The only person who could sign the death certificate was Mother Palmer's daughter-in-law, Gladys Palmer, so much of the information was missing about Danny. He was buried at Fairmount Cemetery.

December 18, 1928
The day after the funeral

Dear Hank,
 They say you are better this morning. I'm sure glad guess I'll get out today. I'm anxious to see the kids myself. Be careful and don't worry too much. I'm going to let your folks know. I got a letter from Mrs. Kaestner, she is so sorry and didn't mean a thing by her letter. I'll send this letter and hers over to your ward and I'll send this tablet and envelopes. You can get stamps from the office. I want to get hold of the baby and kids. I love you dearly and do everything to keep coming on top. Love, Rose

 Hank recovered and so did Rose, but the baby, was now two years old, had so much trauma that he had to learn how to walk, talk and feed himself all over again.
 Shirley took Danny's death very hard and now took it upon herself to spend all her time with baby Vern, teaching him to walk and talk all over again.
 Hank couldn't get back to Eads to work his homestead, so he asked his brother Martin to farm it for him. It seems that the Great Depression was upon them.
 Rose was still in a leg cast, which made taking care of the baby very difficult. Shirley took on most of the household chores as well as looking after the other children.
 Rose took time to catch up on her letter writing. She was long over due answering Ruth's last letter.

Sept. 26, '29

Dear Ruth,
 Your letter received some time ago. Terrible I wait so long to ans. I just can't write it seems. I'll try and ans. some of your quest. about the family. Janet and I decided we wouldn't tell you Aunt Rosalie's add. for she does tell some wild things that make us boil, but you're old enough and got sense enough, that if she ever tells you anything you can believe what you feel you ought. Aunt Rose lives in Sedro Woolley, Wash. Name—Mrs. Rosalie L. Hayden, Lawrence Gillis lives Anacortes, Wash. Ernest

Gillis lives Sedro Woolley. Uncle Walter in Shanghai, China. Mother was born Three Rivers, Quebec, Canada of Scotch Canadian Parents. Grandfather Gillis came from Scotland. Grandmother was Canadian and looked like a Duchess. Father was born at Paulding, Ohio. His parents both Swiss. John can tell you about their ancestors. I can't spell the names. Aunt Ida B. Clem and children are our only relatives on Father's side living. Aunt Ida's children are Hyma, Effie, Lora, Fred, Wendell, Earl, Nancy and Rose. Hyma's name is Mrs. Frederick Cooper. Soo Saint Marie, Ont., Canada. She's a dear. If you are any way near her ever look her up. You were too little to remember her when we lived in Soo Saint Marie but she remembers you. She has a girl as old as you called Ida Lou. We are all white and no bad blood I mean diseased blood that we know. I'm going to try and get Aunt Ida B. to come visit me after the first of the year. It will be nice to have her.

Well, how are all of you. I got a letter from John. He didn't say he was going to get married but he said he was coming to see me this fall. I hope he does get married as he is old enough and he will be settled for life if he married. Otherwise, when he gets old you know how it would be. I got a letter from Janet too. They all have had colds. Well Ruth I will close. Write again soon. Don't wait for me to write. I've got a picture of Father's sister who died. Elizabeth Reuter. I'll send it to you. The weather is beautiful here. Hank's branding calves today but they all have been cutting corn and filling the silo. Donald drove the stacker team this summer. Made a $1 a day. He was awfully proud. Well, Bye.

Love to all of you, Rose

***

In the fall of the year the chokecherries were abundant. They grew along the roadside ditches and fields. It wasn't easy picking them because the ditches were deep, and you would slip on the loose dirt. Sometimes you would encounter rattlesnakes. Rose made chokecherry jelly and chokecherry wine. This was the time of prohibition, so she had to keep it quiet and not mention why she used so much sugar.

The Kaestners came to visit and wanted to pick chokecherries to take home, so Rose and Hank took them to the ditch bank where they were most abundant.

When Rose started to put on weight and look halfway healthy, it was a sure bet she was expecting again. In the spring of 1930 she gave birth to another boy. He was a breach baby; they named him Gerald Ellis.

It seems ironic that nine months after the chokecherry picking episode, Mrs. Kaestner gave birth to her son one day after Rose gave birth.

In June, Shirley graduated from the eighth grade and the picnic was held in Roxborough Park among the massive red rocks. This was a beautiful area for picnics. There were about eight graduates from Castle Rock High School and their families

As if Rose didn't have enough to do, she got a letter from her brother John. He was living over a grocery store in Santa Fe, New Mexico. He met and married his wife Malissa, in Kansas and had this chance to buy the grocery store. His wife was going to have a baby in the fall. John wanted Shirley to come live with them so she could take care of the baby when it came. Since he owned the grocery store, he would always be close by. Three months later Shirley left for Santa Fe.

Rose and Hank needed a bigger house so they moved to an old two story farm house at the entrance to Roxborough Park. A school bus would pick up Doris and Don at the front door. Vern wasn't old enough to go to school yet, but he wanted to ride the bus, so one day he got on the bus with Don and Doris and rode it to school. Rose was frantic, she couldn't find Vern anywhere. She spent hours looking for him. Later the bus driver brought him back home and asked Rose if she was looking for this little boy.

There was a family in Denver that loved the chokecherry wine, and Rose kept them sufficiently supplied. Occasionally, the revenuers would find out about a still in this location, and six or seven black cars would go zipping past into the park. Rose kept her wine hidden in the attic. She was always afraid that they would raid her house, but they were more interested in organized crime.

Shirley wrote quite often. Malissa had a boy, born October 16, 1930. It had been a difficult birth and Malissa was very weak. They named him Charles Frederick Reuter. When he was two, Shirley came back home.

Shirley was a welcome sight. June of 1932 Rose gave birth to a girl, named Olive Marie.

Hank heard about a share crop in Franktown, and by the time the baby was a year old they were moving to the new place. They had some cows and horses, and they planted fields of beans. Shirley took charge of the children, and Rose and Hank worked the fields, plowing and planting. Don was sent to bring in the cows. They had a border collie that was a big help in bringing them in. Don had very poor eyesight and couldn't see the cows. He was scolded for being so stupid.

Rose drove the children to school over roads that were like a roller coaster, just one dip after another. Flintwood school was between Elizabeth and Franktown. Most of the time they would go to Franktown to buy staples. They had a charge account at the corner store.

Shirley had to go to Castle Rock for school so she boarded with the Jewett's. The roads were impassable during the winter snows.

Hank had been putting up with Rose's nagging, but she seemed to get worse the longer they were married. Shirley walked into the barn one day and Rose had badgered Hank to the point that he almost threw a pitch fork at her.

It looked like they might make a go of this place, Don got a bicycle from the catalog that had to be put together. The younger boys got toys, and Ollie got a doll. Shirley and Doris got new dresses and black patent leather shoes.

This was the time of hoboes. They would walk from the railroad tracks hoping to get a hot meal from the farmers. Usually they were given a bowl of beans and some bread, and they were on their way again.

Rose was always glad to see the Watkins man. She bought real vanilla, liniment and spices. The liniment was good for man or beast. It is a mystery where the money came from to buy these items.

CHAPTER 9

THE GREAT DUST BOWL 1930

The Great Dust Bowl of the thirties, destroyed the crops on the prairie. Hank's brother, Martin, wrote that the crops were devastated, and there would be no money from Hank's homestead. They were lucky to be able to hang on through this horrible blight.

Hank wrote back and gave Martin the entire one hundred and sixty acres, to be added to his own. He didn't want any part of farming in Eads. In fact he was fed up with farming, period. The Great Depression was on. He was having a tough time of keeping the share crop in Franktown. They didn't have any money for seeds and were in debt to the government. He didn't know how he was going to pay the corner store in town for the supplies they had charged. Times were bad. Hank and Rose decided it would be better to try and find work closer to Denver.

Hank's brother Martin wrote to tell them about the death of their mother, Carrie Stacia Fribley Kirby, she had died of heart failure. They couldn't afford to make the trip to Eads, but they piled all the kids into the car and off they went.

Martin inherited all of his mother's property and assets. Rose and Hank had a big fight about the land that Hank had given to Martin. She felt that Martin should have at least given Hank the mineral rights to the property. Martin agreed to give him mineral rights to forty of the eighty acres. As soon as the papers could be drawn up he would mail them to Hank.

On the trip back to Franktown, Rose nagged Hank constantly about not standing up for his rights, that he would give the shirt off his back to a stranger, but he wouldn't lift a finger to help his wife or kids. A couple of times Hank would get so angry the car almost went off the side of the road into a wash. The snow was very deep on both sides of the road and any sudden move would bury them.

They stopped in Kit Carson to tell Janet and Ira about Mrs. Kirby's death, but they had already heard about it. News travels fast on the prairie. Earlier that day the road to the ranch had been plowed, and it was still frozen, but very rough. Janet felt bad that they couldn't attend the funeral, but the roads were just too bad to get out. It was February and they had high drifts between them and the main road. She fixed them a meal and sent them on their way before darkness set in.

When they got back to Franktown, they started packing up to leave the farm.

Sam Y. West was a government agent for the farming commission. He told Hank about some land near Sixth Avenue and Kipling, in Jefferson County, that needed some one to manage it. He was to contact a Mr. Hough. It was a fifty-fifty agreement to share the harvest for a one-year lease. It came with a house big enough for his family. It was a two-story frame house with a large kitchen and a big wood burning stove. The property also had a barn and seven reservoirs. The majority of the crop was planted in strawberries. The rest was alfalfa. Next to the house was a large apple orchard.

Mother Palmer heard about the move and told Rose she could work for her one or two days a week if that would help them get on their feet. Rose would take Ollie with her to Mother Palmer's while the older children were in school and during the summer.

The boys had fun playing in the nearest reservoir when school was out. They built a raft and anchored it out in the middle, then they would swim out to it. The younger kids floated on inner tubes next to the edge.

The summer of 1936 Ruth and Edward Stowe came to visit with their children. This was the first time Ruth had seen her sister Rose since she was adopted from the orphanage.

Ruth's son Frederick was six at the time and he was so impressed with the farm that he said he was going to have a farm with a barn when he grew up. He now has fifty two acres in Wisconsin with a beautiful home that he built, but it is a far cry from the farm he saw at the age of six.

***

In the fall, the apples that fell on the ground were made into cider. The old cider press sat in the orchard year round, but it still worked.

The end of the year the share cropping agreement was up and it was either sign up for another year or buy the place for $2800. Well, Hank didn't have that kind of money. *Twenty years later the land was sold to a developer and Levitz Furniture put up their store, there was a hotel and Drive in movie, and restaurants.* He moved the family a half mile to the east, on the other side of Kipling Street, to the Harriman place. It was only about an acre of land.

Hank would have to find a job or farm himself out to work on a more prosperous spread of land.

The children walked to Lakewood School on Tenth and Wadsworth. Ollie was old enough to go to school now, so she walked with her brothers and sister. Part way into the school year, the school notified them they lived outside the district. So the children walked the other direction to attend Daniels School at Simms Street and Colfax Avenue.

The family dog, named "Pup" made all the moves with them all the way from Franktown, sometimes following the last load on foot. He wouldn't get in the car. Hank knew it was too far for him to follow so he picked him up and put him in the back of the car.

Hank got a job on the WPA and Doris was old enough to get on also. President Franklin Roosevelt started this project to give the poor and needy jobs. They built roads and houses for the poor.

Social Security was started in 1935. Hank didn't have much faith in these plans, but he figured he better go along with them, besides he needed the job.

About the time Rose and Hank decided to move from Franktown, Shirley married the preacher's son, Bob Grunwald.

They lived in an apartment near Cherry Creek in Denver. Bob got a job with Woodmen of the World. He was good at figures so it was a good job for him. The letter came with the news that she had a baby in November. They named her Charlotte Linnette Grunwald.

It had been seven years since their last child was born and Rose was ready to give birth to their eighth child. Don was the only one home, at the time, so he had to drive Rose to the hospital in Denver. Shirley and this one were the only ones born in a hospital. It was a girl, they named her Madelyn Ardell. She would already be an aunt when she arrived into this world.

Don was ready to leave home, all he could think about. That's all they needed now was another kid to raise.

Hank wondered how they would pay the doctor and the hospital. On top of everything else, they had to move again. When Rose and the baby came home from the hospital, it was to the new place. This house was smaller, and it was across from the Jewish Cemetery on Thirteenth and Welch Street. The yard was overgrown with hollyhocks and lilac bushes. There was a street car track that ran between Thirteenth Avenue and the cemetery. You could ride it from Golden to Sheridan Boulevard and transfer to another to take you to Denver.

Vern and Gerald would put pennies on the track so the streetcar would mash them flat. It seemed like the kids had pennies and nickels to carry in their pockets, but Rose and Hank didn't have two dimes to rub together.

Somehow Rose found another house to move to by the time the baby was six months old. It was on Twelfth Avenue across the street from Lakewood School on Wadsworth Boulevard. They were back in the school district and much closer for walking.

It was about this time that Rose became interested in reading the *Harlequin Love Stories*. She laid around a lot after having her last baby. She was nursing Madelyn and walked the baby all night long so she wouldn't cry.

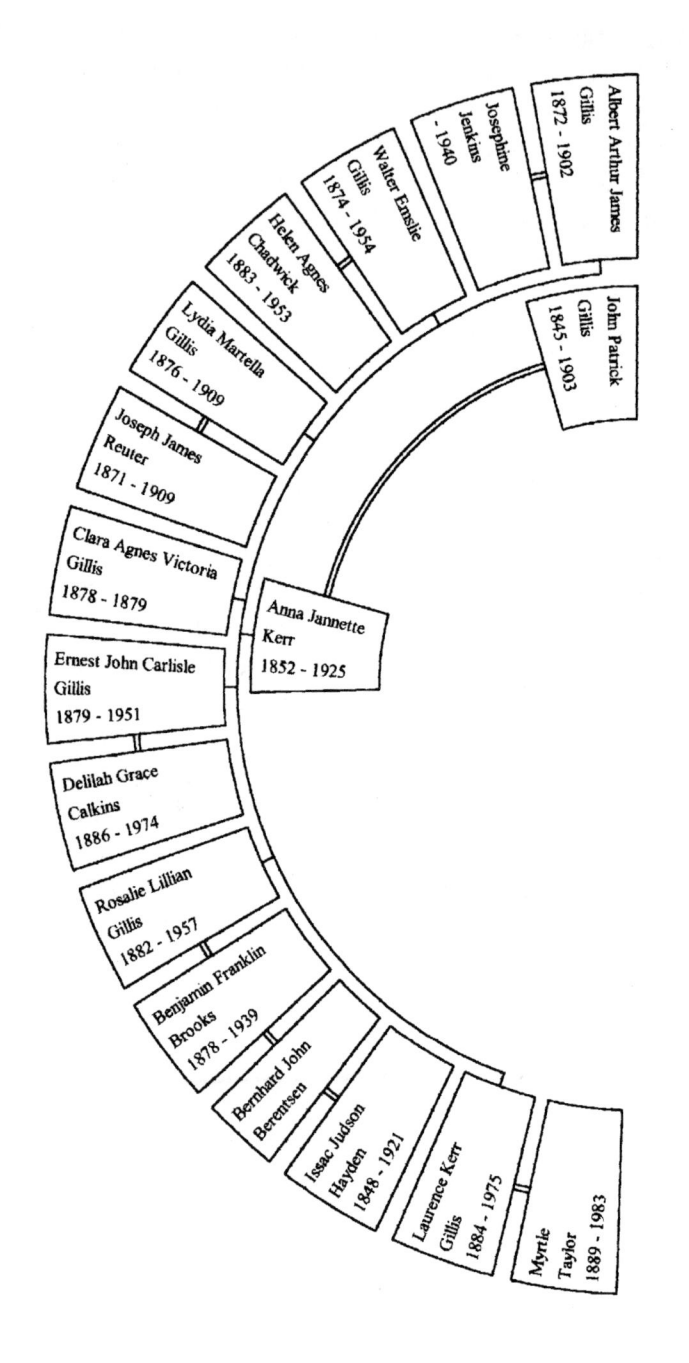

Descendants of John Patrick Gillis

- John Patrick Gillis 1845 - 1903
- Anna Jannette Kerr 1852 - 1925
  - Albert Arthur James Gillis 1872 - 1902
    - Josephine Jenkins - 1940
  - Walter Emslie Gillis 1874 - 1954
    - Helen Agnes Chadwick 1883 - 1953
  - Lydia Martella Gillis 1876 - 1909
    - Joseph James Reuter 1871 - 1909
  - Clara Agnes Victoria Gillis 1878 - 1879
  - Ernest John Carlisle Gillis 1879 - 1951
    - Delilah Grace Calkins 1886 - 1974
  - Rosalie Lillian Gillis 1882 - 1957
    - Benjamin Franklin Brooks 1878 - 1939
    - Bernhard John Berentsen
  - Issac Judson Hayden 1848 - 1921
  - Laurence Kerr Gillis 1884 - 1975
    - Myrtle Taylor 1889 - 1963

Descendants of Frederick Charles Reuter

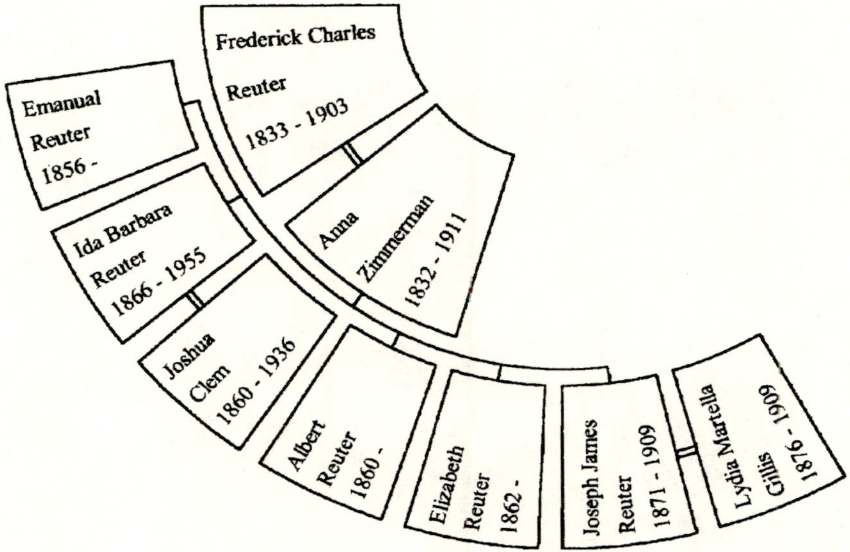

- Frederick Charles Reuter 1833 - 1903
  - Anna Zimmerman 1832 - 1911
    - Emanuel Reuter 1856 -
    - Ida Barbara Reuter 1866 - 1955
    - Joshua Clem 1860 - 1936
    - Albert Reuter 1860 -
    - Elizabeth Reuter 1862 -
    - Joseph James Reuter 1871 - 1909
      - Lydia Martella Gillis 1876 - 1909

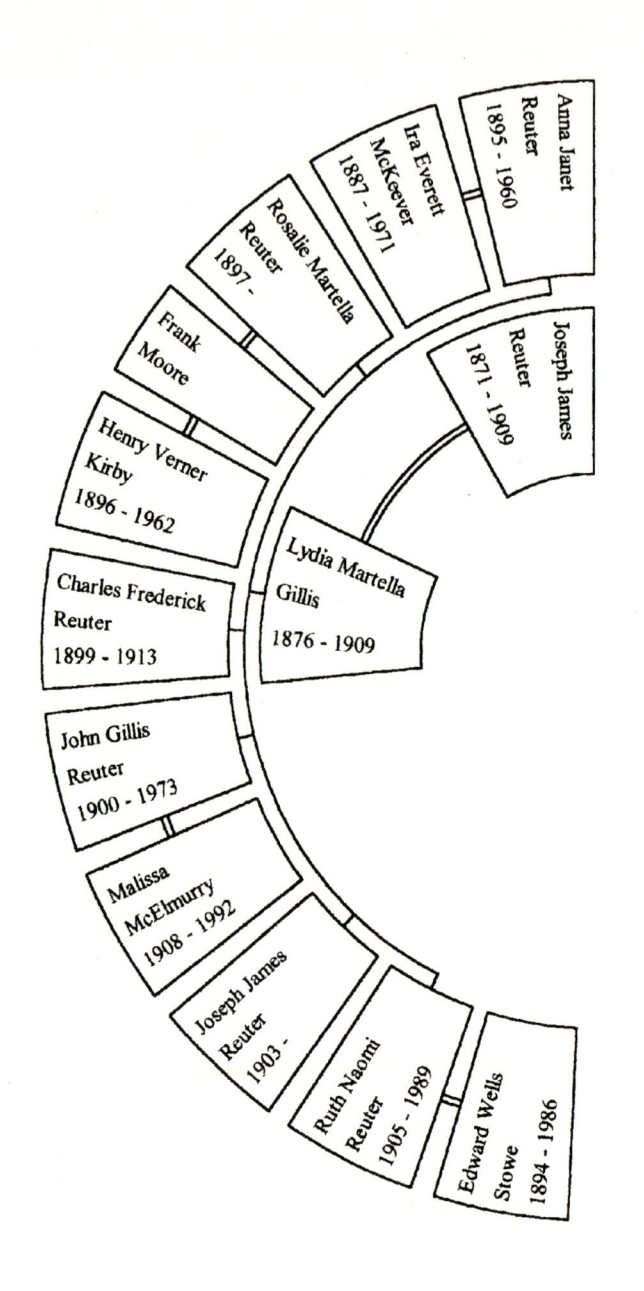

Descendants of Joseph James Reuter

- Joseph James Reuter (1871 - 1909)
  - m. Lydia Martella Gillis (1876 - 1909)
    - Anna Janet Reuter (1895 - 1960)
      - m. Ira Everett McKeever (1887 - 1971)
    - Rosalie Martella Reuter (1897 -)
      - m. Frank Moore
      - m. Henry Verner Kirby (1896 - 1962)
    - Charles Frederick Reuter (1899 - 1913)
    - John Gillis Reuter (1900 - 1973)
      - m. Malissa McElmurry (1908 - 1992)
    - Joseph James Reuter (1903 -)
    - Ruth Naomi Reuter (1905 - 1989)
      - m. Edward Wells Stowe (1894 - 1986)

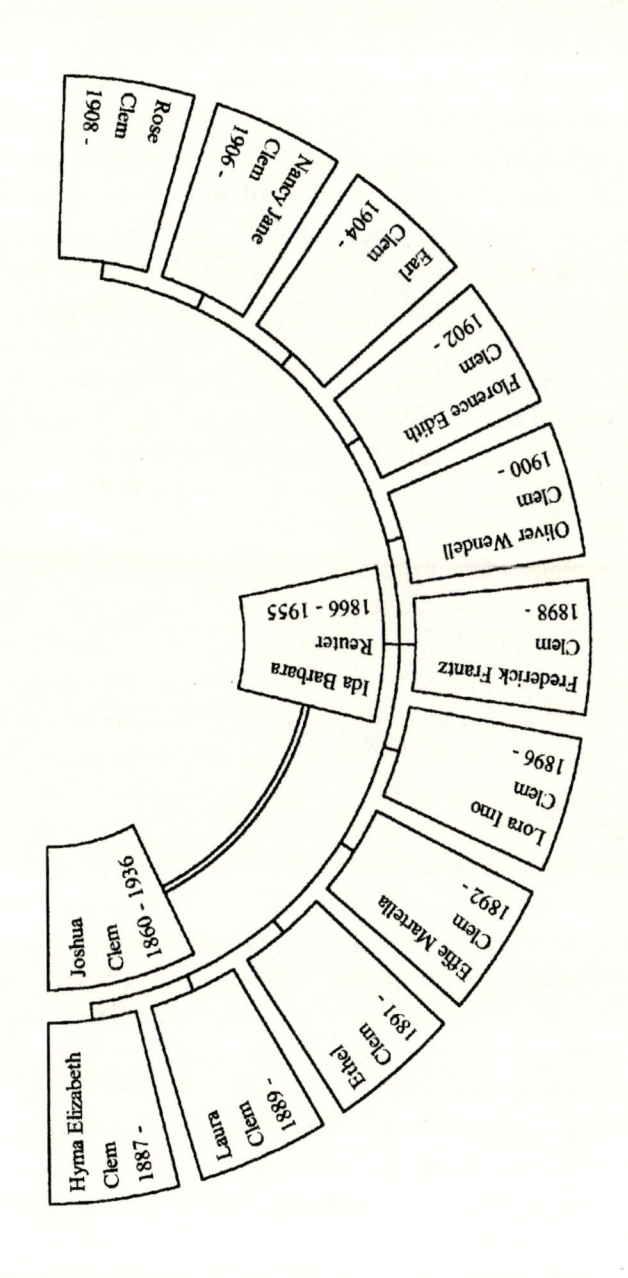

Descendants of Joshua Clem

- Joshua Clem 1860 - 1936
- Ida Barbara Reuter 1866 - 1955

Children:
- Hyma Elizabeth Clem 1887 -
- Laura Clem 1889 -
- Ethel Clem 1891 -
- Effie Martella Clem 1892 -
- Lora Imo Clem 1896 -
- Frederick Frantz Clem 1898 -
- Oliver Wendell Clem 1900 -
- Florence Edith Clem 1902 -
- Earl Clem 1904 -
- Nancy Jane Clem 1906 -
- Rose Clem 1908 -

That is the kind of life she thrived on. She escaped into these books and fantasized her life. It was a disappointment that her daughters didn't lead more colorful lives.

Soon after, Shirley and Bob came to visit and show off the baby. Bob didn't encourage a lot of fuss over the baby, she might catch something. Shirley had a difficult time giving birth, and she was just getting strong enough to get out for a drive.

At this time Doris and Don graduated the same year from high school. Rose didn't want Don going to school by himself, so she held Doris back until Don was old enough to go to school and started them the same year. Everyone thought they were twins.

Don had been working for Richards & Sons Assayers for several months before graduating, and now he could work full time. Doris got a job in Denver as a bookkeeper and rode the street car to work.

The houses were getting better. This one had a basement and an indoor bathroom. There were two bedrooms on the main level, all the floors were hardwood, except the kitchen and bathroom. There were two bedrooms in the basement, where the boys slept.

The front yard had nice grass and trees. The back yard was large but was not sodded. It was a good place to dig in the dirt and make roads and play cars.

Ollie had rhuematic fever and would have severe nosebleeds and sometimes pass out. She had been going to school, but the frequent nosebleeds made her weak, so she had to stay home for the rest of the year. She would start first grade over again next Fall.

While living at this house, Rose's Aunt Ida Bea came for a visit. She didn't stay long and the children wondered where she came from and where she lived. However, they kept these puzzling questions to themselves.

Around Christmas time there was unrest about the war and there was a munitions plant opening up on Sixth Avenue near Howell Road out by Kipling. It was called Remington Arms.

It was time to move again. Rose found a house on Sixth Avenue across from the Lakewood Country Club. Sixth Avenue was a narrow dirt road, and the houses that faced the country club were very nice brick homes, two story with garages and vines growing on the front. It had a large terraced front lawn and a huge back yard, room for a garden. It had a circle drive that went all the way around the house. There were lots of trees and flowers.

The inside was even more beautiful, as you walked in the front door there was a vestibule with parquet floor. From there you could go into the kitchen, living room or up the winding staircase. Upstairs there were four bedrooms and a bathroom with green tile and lavender tub, sink and toilet. One of the bedrooms was small and under the eaves; it was called the attic room.

You had to step down into the living room, which was huge with a fireplace and French windows that cranked out. Off the living room was a glassed-in sun porch quite large; then you had to step up into the dining room from the living room. It had parquet flooring like the entry. Then you could go around into the kitchen. Off the kitchen was a stairway into the basement. It was unfinished, but had very large rooms. The basement held the laundry room with two laundry tubs and next to that was a second bathroom, but it only had a toilet right next to the stoker furnace. The stoker invariably kicked on while you were seated on the toilet. There was a door from the basement directly to the back yard. The garage was attached to the house on the kitchen side. It was one car wide and long enough for two or three cars with a door at both ends.

Rose had to pay seventy five dollars a month to live here, but she had a plan. Men were looking for places to live so they could work at Remington Arms, so she took in boarders and gave them the bedrooms on the top floor. Rose got a job at Remington Arms also. She would cook dinner for them, but they had to get their own breakfast and lunch. They all worked a different shift, so they car pooled to save gas and they all had ration books for shoes, sugar and gas and tires.

Rose put her boys in the sun porch, and she and Hank slept in the basement with baby and Ollie. Doris had the bedroom that overlooked the garage. There were six boarders sharing the other bedrooms upstairs.

Soon Hank left for Pando. There was a job near Leadville, training mules and working on the high mountain passes for military vehicles.

Rose worried about leaving the baby to go to work; there were lots of people in the house at all times. Now that Shirley was married it was up to Doris to watch the younger children.

Apr 18/40
Dear Donald,
Your letter was not only welcome, but came as quite a surprise, as your mother said she did not know if you would write.

I can imagine the work you are doing is very interesting, and I suggest you study mathematics and so forth, even at night if necessary and get more rapid promotion. I have kicked myself quite frequently because I did not finish college. At the time it seemed that the strain of studying and earning a living was not worth it, but since I can see I would have had better positions and perhaps better line of work. However I have seen lots of people with a good education that have not what I have. It is hard to tell just what is best.

The war situation does seem bad, but you are as good a judge of the future in that regard as me. We do not discuss war much. It is not proper for us to do so, because our job is to fight where told, regardless of ideas. We do have far more practicing to do now than we used to before the trouble started. We spend nearly half the time in the field.

It is not necessary for us to have passports to enter border towns in Mexico, but we need visas if we go in more that 14 miles.

I have been to Monterey and Saltillo two times, and I plan on going to Mexico City this fall if I am still stationed here, and if we are not at war. As a rule the Mexicans are a peaceable people, but look rather tricky. I know lots of high class Mexicans both at this side and the other. The Chief of Police here is a Mexican. Of course I do not personally consider them my equal, but I do treat them cordial and they are very nice to me.

Texas has about the worse climate in spring and winter I ever saw. Of course to one coming here from up north it seems ideal, but after you are here awhile you find that "northers" and rain can be very cold an disagreeable. And the weather changes often, just like Feb. it was over a 100 and then last week it got down to 35. Today it is windy and chilly, but tomorrow it perhaps will be near 100. Of course we do have some wonderful weather at times. It seldom snows here, only twice in last 12 years.

I received a letter from your Uncle John today. He says his vacation will be in June, so I'll perhaps be up that way about that time.

Olga is a Dallas, Texas girl, so she thinks Texas is wonderful I kid her a lot about it. She talks real southern.

Shirley wrote me the other day. Her husband looks like a swell guy and the baby is very cute. How do you feel to be an uncle. I can hardly realize I have so many nephews and nieces, but I'll get acquainted with all of you again.

I wish you would come down and stay with me awhile, but know you are too busy there. But later if I get situated in the right town I'll try to let you go to college and stay with me. But that depends on war conditions too.

*Write often, Jo*e

Engineer Section, IX Corps. HQ.
Fort Lewis, Washington
September 26, 1940

Dear Rose,

Was glad to receive your letter a couple of days ago. Sorry to hear that Don was out of work, but perhaps that is for the best. I would suggest that he endeavor to come out here, as there seems to be a lot of activity going on.

Of course I am not in financial condition to actually put out any money on him, What with this continual moving around. However I would be of a great deal of help in getting him situated provided he got here, as I have several contacts with people that are in the "know". From my own experience I have found that the best thing for a boy his age is to get out and rough it, it gives one so much more confidence in himself. It never is satisfactory for some one to advance money and later pay it back. No one can give another actual experience, that must be taken in large doses by the person in question. And experience is what pays the final dividends, not only in cash but in mental comfort. If I was a boy Don's age I would just pack up a few necessities and get out on the road and work a day or so here and there and pay my way to wherever I wanted to go. I do not believe in hitch-hiking or riding the freight trains, it is better to stop at some ranch work chopping wood or anything, get a dollar or so, ride a bus as far as that goes, than work again. It can be done, for that is the way I used to do. In that way he never has to worry about later paying some one back. I feel sure that if he got out here it would not be long until he would be getting located in a good position. Of course there is always the alternative of enlisting in the Army. I do not believe it would be a poor decision for him to do that because there are going to be a lot of promotions in the near future, what with the large expansion. To begin with he would get his board and room, clothes and $21.00 per month, but it is surprising how fast advancement goes these days. I have two men with less than two months service getting $36.00 a month now. This may not seem like much money, but when you figure that it is practically all clear money you can say it is about the same as $100.00 a month in civilian work, and there is good chances for a man of ambition to get $100.00 month by this time next year, if he gets in now.

The main thing is for Don to take the initiative, that is something I can not give him. If he shows the right stuff there is no reason to believe he would not get ahead.

We still fish every day, catch enough to eat. The fact is we have gone on a fish instead of beef diet. Beef is too high for us most of the time.

Write and let me know if Don is coming out, and when to expect him. We will keep an eagle eye out for him. He'll get along O.K. you can be sure.

Love,
Joe & Olga

CHAPTER 10

WORLD WAR II 1940

The war was in full swing and everyone was saving cans, aluminum and newspapers for the war drive. Hank was too old for this war so he didn't have to go. Trucks would come by and pick up the scraps that were used to make ammunition and everything needed for the war. Patriotism was everywhere. Everyone was willing to pitch in to help win the war.

Women were going out to fill the jobs the men held when they were called to the service. Most of the jobs were hard labor, and this was the time for women to wear pants. This started a whole new fashion for women.

Rose wore pants to work at the munitions plant. She was called *Rosie the Riveter*.

There were so many people working at the munitions plant, and Sixth Avenue was the direct route. It was inevitable that the highway department decided that the two lane dirt road had to be widened and paved. Of course the side of the road that was next to the golf course wouldn't be touched. The south side of the street was surveyed and all the houses had to be moved back at least thirty feet. If they couldn't be moved then they were torn down.

92 Engineers
Ft. Leonard Wood, Mo.
Sept 23/41

Dearest Sis,
 Heavens you think I never intend to write again, but I have repeat-

edly asked someone your address, and all they tell me is that you moved. Besides I have been unusually busy since January. Never so busy in my life.

At Ft. Beloved I went to school from 6:00 Am to 8:00 PM, and then when I got to Ft Leonard Wood in Mo. I was busy handling 1100 men until the maneuvers started Aug 4th, and since then we have been on the go continuously in Arkansas and now Louisiana.

It just happens that I am right where I was last May a year ago before we went to California and then Washington. So you see we have been on the go all the time. Olga is following me this time and you can imagine the trouble she is having keeping up with me. For I seldom know when or where we are moving each day., however she has been extremely fortunate in finding me Of course I leave signs along the road to guide our troops and she watches them too. She usually finds a room in a private home to stay, and often gets quite a bit of pleasure out of meeting different people.

I am adjutant of my outfit and so have a great deal of paper work to do in addition to having to pick camp sites ahead all the time. It really does keep me going.

If I had it to do over I believe I would have taken a different type of duty, but the Colonel is an old friend of mine of several years standing he wants me on this job.

At Ft Leonard Wood we have to live 30 miles from the post so it is real tiresome to have to make that drive twice a day after all the other stuff. It certainly is not the ease of former years when I lived right on the post and did about 2 hours work a day.

I haven't had a day off since the first of the year. Really would like to get down to New Orleans while down this far, but don't know yet. I surely was glad to see Ruth as I came through from Wash. DC She really is great, and has a fine family.

I hope to get up there again for a few days, maybe Christmas. But war seems to be getting closer and closer. I may end up in Africa. Don't want that.

Glad Hank and all are getting along so well. Gee, think how time flies. Jeanette to be a grandmother too. Who ever would have thought when I as a mean little brat that I would turn out to be an officer in the Army. But fate takes funny turns. I guess I'll be a Captain next month, so it seems.

You write to me, and I'll be more prompt next time. Best love, Your brother, Joe

Shreveport, La
Oct 15th 41

Dear Rose & Family,
We received your nice newsy letter and we are so proud to hear from you again. and know you are getting allright but sorry to hear of your trouble, you'll just have to try and take care of yourself.

So Doris got married? Know you'll miss her at home so much but you have lots of more lovely ones at home, I know her husband is lucky man. Doris is such sweet pretty girl.

Well Rose your Br. Joe is Captain now got his promotion few days ago. Know you'd be proud of him in his nice uniform as I surely am. He truly deserves it. He works so hard at times and is very ambitious. Think I was very lucky to have found him he's so good to me & I love him dearly.

Do you hear from John and Melisa often? We Haven't heard in some time, but afraid I owe her a letter. I do get so behind with my writing, even to my dear old Dad who's getting so very old, will be 83 22nd of Feb. but I'm trying not to neglect writing him from now on. He writes Joe and I such nice long letters yet.

And Janet is Grand Mother? Was so surprised. Guess she's mighty proud of that baby.

Rose I'll leave my letter open maybe Joe have time to drop you few lines. Do hope you can read this. I'm in bed with light case of Flu. I guess. I just can't seem to get rid of this cold.

Let us hear from you soon.
Love from us both, Olga & Joe

May 10, 1942

Dear Friends,
Received your swell letter OK, but couldn't seem to get around to

answering it as I should. Seems they find something for us to do most of the time. I don't remember whether or not I told you but I am going to school. Studying to be a medical clerk.

We attend school from 8 until 4 every day and drill from 4 to 5. I say every day I mean Monday through Friday. The school is just like high school study periods, typing periods and classes in different kinds of clerks duties. We have several women teachers who treat us like we were first graders, no whispering and if you are caught you are deprived of your recess. So you see it isn't so bad.

The first two weeks we were here we took basic training. Marching, tent pitching and first aid. They really gave us a work out nearly killed most of us off.

You really should be thankful to live in Colorado the dirt blows here nearly every day, it is nearly impossible to keep clean, the barracks and food are full of sand.

Have drawn KP and guard duty three times since I have been down here, and believe me they have no mercy from 6 in the morning till 8 at night continuous. Mrs. Kirby if I were back up there I would never be late for one meal and never dirty a dish unnecessarily.

I surely appreciated the letter, have received several from the boys up at the plant, and as I gather it the new building is nearly ready for operation. As it looks now they can't have too many or too quick to get this thing over with.

Seriously though to date the Army hasn't been so bad. The food has been pretty good and since school has started the drilling g has been limited. The really tough part was the being away from swell people like you folks. There are several Denver boys in our barracks and they are all nice fellows which helps things a great deal.

My wife is very good about writing and telling me the news. She is getting ready to open her beauty shop, she has nearly all her equipment now and has her location picked out so it is a matter of time till she gets under way. I am glad as I figure it things will be pretty tough when this war is all over, especially for the fellows coming out of the Army. I have her all the money I had coming from the plant on back wages which sure helped her out as it made a good down payment. If you ever get down to the Springs, drop into the house and make yourself known she would be more than glad to see you. The address is 24 Cheyenne Boulevard. And don't forget.

I suppose by now the flood damage has been taken care of. According to the papers there sure was a lot of property damage.

If only part of that water were down here to quiet this dirt, then no one would be hurt.

I'll bet Gerald was a proud boy with that new bike, tell him when he gets through with it, to send it to me and save me all this walking.

Has Tommy gone to the Army yet? I wrote Mac a card at Colorado Springs and got a letter in return which I haven't answered yet.

Will close for now, sure appreciated your letter. I hope you will excuse the writing as I am using my bed for a writing desk.

Always your friend, Ivan Sperry

Tullahoma, Tenn.
June 18—42

Dear Janette & Family,

I have some bad news for you, our Joe is being transferred to foreign service, of course we don't know where as yet, I am hoping & praying it won't be too far.

I've been looking for this every day, for two weeks but its such a blow when it does come.

His address in N.Y. will be for a short time only A.P.O. 1099 c/o Postmaster, New York, N.Y. Knew you'd want to write him while he is there.

I'm going to make my home in San Francisco, Calif. with my sister for a while and of course soon as I learn where he's sent will let you know. But I don't look to hear myself for some time, you know how this Army is.

Janette I'm so nervous can't hardly write as you can see, and let Rose know his address as I've lost hers.

My address at my sister's will be 329A Inf. Terrace, Presidio of San Francisco, Calif. I'll be there in about ten days, as I am going to visit my sister in Dallas, also my Dad in Texas. My older sis is going to make trip with me to Calif. which I'm so thankful for.

I'll write you again soon, Love from us both.
Olga & Joe

Aug 8/42
92nd Engs. A.P.O. 508
New York, N.Y.

Dear Rose,

I got your V-letter yesterday, so you see it is not too fat. However I was certainly glad to hear form you. You should feel distinctly honored now because you are the first person other than Olga I have written to since I left the States July 1st.

Of course you can not expect to hear much from me, for there is so little I can write about. We work ten hours a day, seven days a week and I am not allowed to tell you where I am or just what we are doing. I will tell though that I'm a battalion commander now and have about 550 men under me, am set up away from the rest of our regiment, so have plenty to do.

This England is a pretty country, and all sorts of small villages. And most of them are quite snug. I do not know if Hank was here when he was over or not.

It begins to look like we may have to fight yet. I hope it is over soon, for I feel so much like I were in prison way over here away from Olga too. Such is life now.

I am learning to play "darts", an English game and stay close in to camp most of the time. I guess you have seen these "peeps" that is what I use to make inspection trips in, and they are ideal over here.

I am becoming quite a tea drinker. Although I always did like tea. Glad the folks are all getting along OK. How is Shirley? Guess she thinks I've completely forgotten her.

Well, Sis, drop this on to Jeanette for I'm not writing much for the time being. Love, Joe

> Postcard from Carl Ader
> 16th Naval Construction Bat.
> Naval Construction Training Center
> Hueneme, California
> Tuesday, Aug 27/42

Dear folks & Gary,
Am on the go again leaving this place this afternoon. Will arrive in Hueneme, California in about 5 days. How is everybody? Did Tommy ever get in the Air Corp? Suppose he has by this time. Had 5 days leave. Thelma met me in Chicago. Had a good time while it lasted. Write when you have time. Love, Carl

Letters from Pando

> Saturday
> Sept 19-42

Dear wife and kids,
How is things going there? We have been unsettled every since we have been here. Expecting to go home every day and I may beat this letter home. Yet the grub is fare. My cold is better. The only ones that drop dead here are old men with bad hart. And the ones that get nemonia are the ones that get drunk and lay around on the ground. I don't notice any difference in the altitude. There was two hundred forty came up, one hundred 80 got in.
You don't kneed to worry about me up here. All you have to worry about is you and the family. I don't think l will get paid untill next Friday. How is Don doing on his job. We had a skiff of snow this morning, it was cold for a while but warmed up. I will close for this time. Tell me the news. Hank

> Kit Carson, Colo.
> Sept 20, 1942

Dear Rosalie & family,
I expect Dorajean has told you all the news but I want to write and tell you how much I enjoyed your letter. I'm glad you folks and Mary had a good visit Labor Day she wrote me too. Its nice Hank has such

good work at Pando but you'll sure miss him as its not been many times he's been gone so long has it or maybe he'll get down some week ends. Meiers and Jelinicks were close to this work when they were on their vacation.

I'm sorry Vales' friend has gave you so much trouble. I don't think Vale would have taken him there if he'd known how things would work out. Hope you get your board money from him. Let me know if he doesn't pay up. I think Dorajean will jump on him anyway. She's not so meek when she gets started. I'm glad you are having a visit with her and Janet Mae, they are enjoying it so much. We surely hated to have them leave.

I don't think so much of that country southeast of Las Animas but Long may have a very good place. Be sure and let me know if you accept his proposition. That country isn't near as nice as Denver.

Sorry Don didn't pass what he wanted in the glider dept. but it's probably for the best anyway.

I had a letter from John he said he was still going to school. I also had a letter from Lee Ramsey he just got back from Alamosa where he attended his grandfather Liles funeral. Lee is at Fort Devens, Mass. He said it was so far coming and going he didn't have much time to visit.

We've had feed cutters since Tuesday sure is a heavy crop. We had our first killing frost last night had quite a lot of ice. The four men including Ira Jr. put up 126 shocks of feed on 8 acres yesterday with about 20 bundles to a shock. The Hogan boys say it will make 35 But of grain to the acre. Tell Madaline I think she's a sweet little girl and kiss her for me. I'm glad she likes Janet Mae.

Well I must close for now and get busy. Write me soon and tell me all the news. Love to all from us all

Ira, Janet & Ira Jr.

PS Tell Doris I wish her all the good things and will try to get a present sent her soon. I've not heard from Shirley since you were down. Those cherries and raspberries were the best ever.

Sept 21—42

Dear husband,

Need I say I miss you? Baby started this letter to you. We got your letter today and very glad to hear. My I had a time with baby when it got so late and you never came. She said Mom where's daddy we got to go get him. Her face went panic as if we had misplaced you. The first news to us is that Don's draft card came to report Thur. for physical to Dr. Bailey. He has been summoned to court Wed at 10:00 o'clock. That Royal insurance that we didn't want is sueing for $32.00 . I believe we will get out of it I hope.

I was really worried Hank over your cold. I feel so much better to night about you. Mr. Sloan said that 4 men didn't go up that morning and they are now doing for Uncle Sam in the Army.

Doris is just fine Bob tries so hard to do the right thing.

Don is getting along fine with job. He thinks he gets paid 2 times a month, he don't know.

Vern is alright finally got his hair cut. Gerald is good to me. Olly is missing you as baby is.

I got rid of Bob Moore. But Vale never gave him up. Vale was fired this morning. We would not know but Don was at Lakewood Cleaners at noon today and Vale & Bob were sitting by the Drug Store. Don ask them how things were going they said they had been fired, it is now 9:45 and Vale has not come home yet. I'm expecting something but what I do not know. Think of us Hank but don't worry to bad about us, there may be many changes when you come back.

I had to go up and try to calm Dorajean so have delayed this letter. It is now 11:30 Vale has just come in and what excuse I do not know. I'll put a P.S. in the morning.

I got a letter from Bro. Joe, in England he wondered if he was tramping on ground you tramped.

You got a bond today and also a refund of $4.05 I signed your name to it and you know that is the first time I ever did that.

I picked the pumkins & squash put in garage for time being. I have to order some hen scratch right away. Melons didn't ripen. I'm going to take a butcher knife and open them. Chickens eat every bit of them. Mrs. Friedian sent me a bu basket of sand hill plums. I've been making jelly and it really is good. I'll be put in jail for such a thing but I can't throw them out.

Mrs. Wilkins was over Sat. evening to visit me Mrs. Sloan and Bonnie Lou all at the same time. Don sure is getting disgusted with them.

Hank take care of yourself. We all miss you and wish you were here. I'll do my best here till you get back. Tell me if I should mail your clean shirts to you. Do you want me to mail you cigs, candy or money. Love from us all

Rosalie

P.S. I'll write you Vale's excuse next time if it is interesting Norman says it wont be the truth anyway. R.

While Hank was working at Pando in Leadville he was making $1.50 per hour as a jack hammer operator. He stayed in the Vandome Hotel in Leadville.

His contact there was H.E. Bergland.

Sept-24-42

Dear Hank,

How are you? I'm sending you up a package hope you get it as your two shirts are in it. Don't try to wash send them down dirty. Things are sure happening but no answering yet so will write later about them. Vale says he wont work if he has to do common labor. They both know how I feel about it. He pretends he is looking. Don took physical this morning. He is now seeing a lawyer he got stuck on that Royal Indemnity Co. for $32.00 and court costs.

He don't get paid till Oct 1st and he says they keep one weeks pay. He thinks he will be in Army by 1st.

Do you get the Denver Post up there? Doris is still fine, we hope and hope things will calm down before she has to go so she can rest. I work night and day to get tired enough to sleep and it meets me again in the mornings.

Take care of yourself and come home to me as soon as you can. I feel it is a job we have to do, so am really trying to. Our kids are grand. Each does their part.

Its heck we had to go to army first and that darn Vale struts over town.

Well Hank write me and be sure you tell me if you get your shirts. Doris sent candy as I have no way getting candy till you come home. Everybody here is well. Lots of love Hank Rosalie

Friday night
Sept-25-42

Dear Daddy,
    Your Tuesday letter arrived and I do feel a lot better when I hear and you sound like you can take it. Do you really think they will make you a drain layer? Bobby says he wants to see Leadville and what it looks like up there and as bad as I would like to see you I'm afraid I will have to discourage them as Doris may be effected by the altitude, I took her over to Arvada today she was to see her Dr.
    He says she may not go longer than 3 weeks. I made Don take her down town last week, we don't let her out of our sight.
    Don has decided not to sue it seems better to pay what has to be and take it.
    I paid the water bill today. Baby says to tell you she had some candy today. Norman comes back tomorrow. Vern is quitting Friedian this Sunday so he says, I sure hate Marvins influence on him. Don is sure good around here and can eat a full lunch pail now. He has raised to a dollar an hour now. It's a shame that darn war. Gerald has a sore finger acted like that thumb did so I started soaking it. I think it is quite a bit better.
    Yesterday 24th was Janet Mae's birthday and Vale promised to be home, he hasn't any job. Well he didn't come and he didn't so I called C. Patrol and no reports and I called Police Dept. and no news there so today he came in at noon with Bob and another boy 17 yrs old. The car is sure smashed up he says he had a wreck last night at 9:00 you know where that curve is on Colo. Boulevard out by Derby. Well he was going so fast he couldn't make it and went over that high embankment.
    It's sure a mess. We wanted him to see a doctor but, no. He's been in bed rest of day. He can't hunt work tomorrow and Sun. isn't any good so he will have to wait till Monday to start out again. He didn't call the Police nor Patrol he spent the night with Bob on Larimer St. He isn't

out of trouble yet as he don't own car and insurance wont do anything unless they have a police report. I hate like the dickens to take up paper with their darn mess.

You take care of yourself for me and write me as often as you can. I am glad you saw Bill Stutz. I would like to be a booby and cry for you to come home but I wont, if you can take it I can and I'm going to have a treat when you do come. Do you stay at barracks or at Leadville?

Lots of love Rosalie

Sept-26-42

Dear wife and family,

I got your package today. Thanks a lot for everything. You don't kneed to send me any sugar I've still got the can I brought with me. I appreciate candy and cigs but if you have any money to spare get yourself something. They have a store here I can buy anything I want if I stand in line for one or two hours. But I don't kneed anything but smokeing.

I got paid today for two days $27.22. My first meal ticket ran out today and I got another one that will last till next Saturday. I paid for two out of this check. Then I will only have to buy one ticket out of the next check and I will send you the rest. Can you get along till then? I should have a pretty good check next Friday. I haven't figured it up yet but I haven't worked less than 12 hr days this week and I got three 14 hr days and one 15 hr day and 7 day weeks. $17.00 per day for 14 hrs. $21.00 per day for Saturday and Sunday. I should get a check from B and G for two days it may be sent to you if it comes at all. I've got $5.80 left if you kneed it I will send it. I'm sorry you've got such a mess with Vale. I hope Bob don't come back. Vale could get a job up here if he would. This is open shop he wont have to join the union. The Pando Construction Co will hire men at the gate and pay union scale and ask no questions. I didn't have to bring any bed they furnish that to and plenty of it. The barrocks will be pretty nice when they get them finished. There will be shower, bath and toilet in each one. The camp is about 3 miles long and 1/2 mile wide and hundreds of barrocks all ready built. They also have mule barns for 10,000 mules. I have been drilling rock up there with jack hammer. We are working for Peddicord Con. Co. But in a separate group. B and G has no contract here. Tell the kids hello and goodnight.

Love to all from Hank

Monday night
Sept 28-42

Darling,

What are you doing? Are you still working long hours? Did you mail money down Friday? Mrs. Westerfelt gets hers on Monday. I'll let you know just as soon as I get it. I will only wish you were coming with it. Aren't any coming down? Is Saturday and Sunday time and a half?

This is sure getting me down I'm so everlasting tired and Doris is planning on me being at the Hospital when she has the baby. I was thinking last night what would I do with my baby. Dora Jean don't care about my baby too much. I do hope Vale gets a job that pays enough to rent them a room. He is hauling coal today.

They have raised the price of lunches at school. 40 cents a week hereafter and they start Wednesday.

I can't work till Doris is over because I have to be here to take her to the Hospital. I haven't been able to pay Ferguson a cent since you left. He don't smile so sweet. Do you want me to send you back some money for your expenses? Be sure Hank and tell me if you got package. Would you rather I didn't send cigarettes. I thought maybe it would keep you from standing in line.

Honey I'm still waiting for my treat when you come home, I reach out to touch you and you aren't there. Are you well? Do take care of yourself. I'll manage some how here. Say Hank Mr. Westerfelt don't cash his check up there he sends the check, she sends him what he needs. You do what you want. Next time you go on a job I'm going too. I don't own any home or house I have to be tied to and this mess I am in now is plain munching. You know that big sow Ira had it brought $68.85.

Darling do you have a time reading my writing? I love to get a letter from you. Write me everything and I love you.

Monday night (later)
Sept 28-42

Dear Hank,

    I shut chickens up tonite I'm going to have to buy feed as soon as I can they are too big to trust running around anymore. There are only 37 of them and they are all big enough to eat. I'm not eating any of them till you come home. Gerald and I took the little coop out of chicken yard so they can't fly over, we hope!
    I got 1 bu. of grapes $2.00 Saturday. I made juice, can either drink or make jelly out of it. I got 1 bu. of delicious apples this morning from Mrs. Speck, also. Don does my running for me. That is all the canning Hank I'm going to do. It's an awfull lot to start moving around. Bobby came home all hepped up. He wasn't going to go back to work to morrow. And Doris is in no state to take anything. I stepped in but he feels he is getting a raw deal, but who isn't? He threatened to join army tomorrow if she wouldn't let him go back on railroad. I told him not to start her living under a threat every time he didn't get his own way. He was tired and is tired. You see they promised him an excavator for a truck when they re-classified their men out there and they didn't they just left him a helper. I told him he wasn't ready then. I think he will go back to work to-morrow he's been very good so he has to blow up a little.
    I have taken two aspirin tonite hoping to sleep. It isn't hard to do for our family cause I like then as well as you do and I feel as long as you have to put up with what you do, I can to. But my working out is out till you come back. I can't leave Olly and baby a moment with Doris. But I also make her feel she is very important right now. I am sick Hank when I think of what she has to go thru yet. Shirley is about 6 months. Yet I have no time for her at all. Write me I live to hear from you. Love me Rose

Tuesday
Sept 29-42

Dear Daddy,

    I just received your letter this noon sure we can manage. I let Don have five for a lawyer and had $15.00 dollars for gas & lights but when your letter came I just told Ferguson what you told me and asked if I could string a long if I gave him the $15.00. He said we could manage.

I'm sure glad to hear from you Hank. You write a nice letter we can picture you up there. My where are they going to get the mules? Norman said he knows a man who has 20. My mailman says Vale can get in serious trouble for moving that car before the insurance Co. said he could. No one was involved but himself so he says. So the cops don't have anything on him. Well the quickest way is to see what comes next.

Kenny soloed yesterday. (I am sending another one). I'm sure glad you like the package I can send another but I don't have another shirt to send you. Why don't you roll up some dirty ones and mail down in that shoe box it don't take long to get here. All is still well with Doris, Bobby went back to work today.

I read your letter to Don an Doris, Dora Jean heard she said it was just as well where Vale was now. He hauled two loads of coal yesterday

No, no check came from Broderick & Gordon except the $4.05 from your bond. No I don't need your change. I'm only sorry you didn't take enough money to take care of it, what did you do borrow for your first ticket? Five chickens flew over that fence with nothing to stand on but the ground. Don't worry about how I manage here. I will take my spree when you can be here with me, I'm made queer that way. As soon as I can see day light I am getting my permanent as my hair is terrible now and if I want a permanent I'll have to keep it as long as it is. I want to get one before Doris goes to the hospital.

Vern found another job after school hours. I don't feel bad about him quitting the plaster business, you know what bad colds he had last winter.

Gerald went over to caddy tonight. This is just about all the news except Hank, I feel 100% better since I got your letter. It is sure heck what will pop up next here.

There has been no further notice of Don's draft notice but they say they are taking another bunch of boys Oct 15th. Shirley is 26 the 17th of Oct.

Take care of yourself, if you get sick come home. You sure sound like you are putting in time. Love me, Rosalie

P.S. Ferguson brought baby a nice sack of candy today. I am mailing some more cigs up to you. Love Rose

Tuesday nite

Vale got in two more loads today. Johnny is working on jack hammer for Launmier Load Meyer or something like that.

Mrs. Ader called up tonight and said Mac could come out and wanted to but he didn't want to bother me with supper but I want Mac to come he is bringing Grace Sulivan too and Mrs. Ader, Thursday nite around 8 or 8:30. He works long hours too.

I have your cigarettes in house will get them off in mail. Bobby came home a little more cheerful.

Vern's job is with two old maids, he is to vacuum the rugs to-morrow. He worked all the time after school they paid him 20 cents as tho he was a little boy. It's going to do him good to get out a little and see what some people really do. Don is putting some gas in both cars for fear of a shortage soon.

I went out to put chickens in that got out and only 3 came to gate unless some flew back in. It only makes 33. I sure don't want to kill a pullet. We are not getting eggs now except at Fergusons, Nora's hens aren't laying. I'll leave my letter open so if I think of anything I'll put it down. Are you able to read it?

Baby has a fear I'm going to come up missing too. Sometimes she crys loud when she can't find me right a way. Isn't she sweet? Do you have electricity. I hope it don't take to long to finish that job. The next one I promise you I'm going on.

Wade's were over Sunday nite. They said tell you Hello and that they missed, thought everything was fine.

Well it is a grand day, Infantile Paralysis broke out in Torrington, Wyoming, well I will close Write me whenever you can. Love me Rosalie

Monday nite
Oct.—42

Dear wife and family

I got your letter today we sure glad to get it. I hadn't got one for four days but I guess you are to tired to write. I don't blame you any. I had to go back on the hammer Sunday morning. One hammer man got the same as I had and had to go home, another had to go home to move so that left only me. I guess I will be on from now on. Yes I really do feel good untill today I was pretty loggy. We had some hard drilling in granit rock. I am up high in Eagle Canyon the road that goes across to Climax. I haven't found any one to come home with yet I can't hardly take a whole day off now. I just talked to Allen he said about two days next week would finish us up so I may not be home till then. We had some bad weather but it is nice again now. I found the stamps they were in a new envellope. There were three. They may last while I am up here, I hope so. I don't get up to the store anymore it is so far to walk. I've got my feeling back again hope you don't lose yours. I hope those tires are good and not to high I will write again Friday. Love me. Hank

Thursday evening
Oct—42

Darling
    I got your letter! I feel a lot better. Don't know how you will like it but Hank the U.P. called up and wanted to see me so I went down passed inspection took my physical and go to work 8 in the morning hrs from 8 to 4 everyday of week, I'll be told which day I have off. 48 hr week. Time and a half for overtime and 10% has to be taken out for bonds. They warned it would be real hard work. Inside and out. Maybe I can get worn out enough to sleep nights then. Maybe the days will go faster. I should not leave Doris but they may not call again and untill you come home I can't stand to see Dora Jean this and that. I have warned them that nothing is important except my baby being happy. So because I was going to work I got Gerald pair over shoes, 3 buckle. They have to walk to school you know. What a day to get me a job. Rain and the basement is full of water. I did the washing to night so the girls would not be over taxed. My problem is going to be getting to work and back.

The last appraiser was here he said it looked like we would be moving about middle of winter.

I'm going to try and stay awake till Don comes he sure got a bawling out from Barbara and he bawled her right back. He is pretty near crazy with his teeth besides his worries. His system can't stand his teeth being pulled yet.

Well when your clothes come I'll send them to laundry and see what can be done. I'll mail you clean right back then I suppose by this time you have your other suit of underwear. Say wasn't that queer mixture in those packages of candy?

Baby and I were planning on making a date with you, we were going to take bus up there but now we don't know. I'll know soon what day I have off. We miss you and I do love you. I'll be careful Hank how I act. And maybe I wont have to work when you come home. I really could of enjoyed being kept if you had been home. Are you taking out 10% bonds? I have to get ton of coal again. Boy it sure is pouring down. Love me. Rosalie

P.S. I'll write you tomorrow night how work went and also pay. I really don't know yet. Norman joined the army. I forgot to tell you.

Friday nite
Friday
Oct 2-42

Dear wife and family,

How are you all. Have you still got your mess? I hope not. Be sure you let me know a few days before Don has to go so I will have time to get there.

Well this is pay day but I didn't get my check. They told me I would have to come back tomorrow. I wanted to get it in the male to nite so you would have it by Monday.

Bill Yoder's wife came up last nite and he went back with her for a weak. He has been runing the compressor for me. I will be drilling rock on the ski corse tomorrow. Four miles up the mountain. I didn't stay with the drain layers long. I don't think I will get any more 14 hr. days. It is dark by 8 o'clock. My check this week if I get it all will be $123.50.

I will have to have $10.00 of that for a meal ticket. I will send you the balance. I saw Johnny Ferguson several days ago. He is running a jack hammer for the Loudermilk Bros.

We had a little rain this evening it settled the dust. I sure feel a lot better too. A lot of sick men are leaving everyday. There are not many of us left. 8 of the drain layers that quit came back last nite for less money than they were getting they said they hadn't made a cent since they left here. Have you heard from Mr. Long yet. There is a roomer that B and G will have a big job at Buena Vista after we get thru here. That will be a tank testing ground that will be a good go for us.

I will send you a money order in this letter tomorrow. Love to all, Hank

P.S. Well I wrote more this time than I suposed I could think of in a week. Well, don't know what to write now so I will close for this time. Yours truly with lots of love. from H.V.K.

Oct 2—42

Dear Hank,

How are things going? Are you well? Baby misses you so. Well hell's been popping here. The Constable and Chief of Police came yesterday with an attachment on the car. They had orders to take car in to garage at Golden then Don would have to go back to court to get car back. Well we sure had a time as we all here were stoney broke. So I had to borrow $39.00 from Mrs. Wilkins to keep the car from going out the gate. The day before that the gas & electric man wouldn't leave without shutting off electricity, till I paid him. I went down to bank and drew out Vern's money and paid that.

I've turned down two darn good jobs. I can't take a chance on Baby being left alone right now. Doris is fine. Kids are all well. Vern wishes you were home. Have you learned how long you will be yet?

Broderick & Gordon is taking over at the Arsenal out at Derby, so I heard, in three weeks.

The appraisers were here to find the value of the house. One of them was Mr. West. Our house is second block. The 1st Block of road bid was opened. Monohan Road Construction got the job.

Vale quit his coal hauling job 2 days off then he found another. He is now an iceman, 57 cents and hour. Vale got out of car deal without having to pay anything. The wrecker came to day to drag it away. Mac, Sully and Mrs. Ader were here. He works at Arsenal, steel construction. He hasn't long to work as he has enlisted in the Navy. He is a Petty Officer. Is waiting for his call.

It was sprinkling a little tonight. Write me when you can. Tell me everything. If you get sick come home. I'm glad you are yourself Hank. I don't have to worry about you. Come home safe to us.

Don brought me home a queer kind of candy stuff. Got it down at Joslin's. I will send you some in your next package. Send your dirty clothes down. Gosh I'm everlasting tired if I ever get off I don't know what I would do to get rested. You must be tired too the hours you put in. Well, I will go to bed now Honey good night? Wish you were here.

Ford Fox's gang all came back they said they couldn't stand it. Sam West knows Ford Fox real well. Mr. Sloan is very interested in wondering what Mrs. Kirby will have to take next. Don Reeves quit his job in Utah. Martella called up tonight. They just got here today.

Don took a nail out of tire you got from Bob. Inner tube tore to pieces.

Well Hank good night. I love you, Rose

Saturday morning. Well I saved a little space to put in any other news. Vale insists on staying away from work. On this ice wagon he don't have to be down there till 10:00 and don't get home till 10:30 at night. He says he don't want any job where he has to get up in the morning. Well can you read my writing? I have found a tent. That tire that was punctured yesterday is flat today.

Do you get tired hearing of our troubles. Well I do to. I've never been so hard up since before I started work the first time. Are you taking out 10% in bonds yet? Maybe you had better. Do you have what you need, anything I should send you? Be good. Love me, Rose

Monday nite

Oct. 5—42
Dear Hank,

Your money arrived and thank you gosh it was a nice check. Well I am working but for one purpose, just to move about where you work. Say if you get a chance to come down, Come Down. I know the money is valuable but we have always considered that and missed a lot.

I would come up with my baby but you know why I can't right now. I gave $70.00 to Ferguson $8.64 telephone and paid the debt to Mrs. Wilkins. Don is going to help me on that. He don't get paid but every two weeks. I will take up a few more bills then.

You know that man called Morey we met over at Joe Riley. He went up the week you did, plumbing inspector, he only stayed a week. He got a severe cold and had to come down. Joe got layed off at the Arsenal and was as good as drafted to that job in Neb. near the South Dakota line but he is not going unless he simply has to. He is trying to get a job out of Don Wilson at Pando. Don Wilson went up today to look the ground over. He is labor commissioner. She feels pretty bad about it.

Don and Martella are back from Utah looking for work. He is considering Pando too. Mrs. Race called me Sunday she is outside of area. You get to their place by going east on Colfax and go in that way some place near K.O.A. You know where. They bought a house 2650 Champa, Negro section, you remember where we used to go hunt up Hoover?

Jack Kimsey has a 22 rifle now. You know that white hen, he killed it.

We have all talked our head off to get Vale to go down and go to Pando. I sent him down to 810 14th St. and he said they didn't trucks they wanted common laborers. He said he wasn't going to do common labor. So he is now and ice man. We have talked now to night and he may go down again to morrow morning and sign up. I think I will go get my hair done real soon. I am a sight. I told baby you told me to get her a brand new cry baby doll for her. She is all lit up about it. She has been pretty sick, is better now but shakey, she fell down basement stairs and hurt her lip. Doris nearly came too trying to catch her. Another batch of appraisers to night again. It makes the third set.

Don stays around to see if you write. We all miss you. Don got his next draft card, he is class 1A. Unless he can find other enlistment, he will be in army soon. Doris is still fine. I will write you Hank as soon as we hear from Draft Board and also when Doris has her baby. I don't want our resentment of Bob to be handed on to her baby.

I am not out of my mess but I can't do much about it. Janet wrote me and asked us to please watch out for Dora Jean and baby that the board may take Vale soon the way he is acting. I've got off this line some way so I will close now and thanks for writing such newsy letter. Love Me?

Honey I sort of will be glad when we can have a life of our own. If it is Buena Vista well and good I'm not glued here. I'm so glad I belong to you and not some one else.

Deer season has opened. Mrs. Sloan is trying to wrangle a bid from Don for Bob Sloan to go hunt in Roxborough Park. I don't know if Tony Helmer will let him.

No never heard a sound from Long yet. Still hoping if you are.

I have 31 chickens now. Mr. Orin Miller called up wanted to know how every one was doing. He sure is a dandy man, he likes us all.

Mrs. C.O. Palmer has been very sick. You know she had that bad leg and excema broke out all over her body. I really ought to call her but I'm afraid she will want me and I hate to leave my baby at mercy of these girls. I got that prescription filled again you know B—ache. Baby sure was bad.

Well night honey, I'll write some more before I close this envelope. *Tuesday Morning.* How are you? Does the dust bother you any? Remember if you don't feel good come down. It wont hurt you to come down for a visit, will it? But do take care of yourself. I'm mailing Zohm $6.00 to day. He will summon us into court as did Orville Dennis. Say Hank Dora Jean acts like she is stationed here. Doris is making plans so that when she is over her baby she and Bob can go by themselves when we are ready to pull up stakes. Well darling write me often. I'm packing another package isn't much but does keep you in tobacco. Is there anything down here you want? besides us I mean . Tell me if you got the other package. Mail dirty clothes down. Love from all of us.
Rosalie

    Especially love from me, Rose

Baby says tell Daddy his little girl needs him. She's sweet.

Tuesday
Oct 6—42

Dear wife and family,

 I got your letter Monday you sure are having your troubles. I hope you got the money I sent by now. Thanks for the cigaretts and candy.

 Yes I do put in long hours but it is nothing to compare with what you have to put up with. I wish I could send you as much money every week as I did last but the days are getting shorter. We are going to work later and quit earlier about 11 or 12 hours is the best I can do. But if I can make 85 or 90 per week besides my bord it will be the best I have ever done. I do hope your trouble will end soon. If I catch someone going to Denver I will go along. Allen and Osborn went down last nite and back this morning. I didn't know they were going until they had gone. They say we are here for two months yet, it is still dry and dusty here the days are warm.

 Early morning is cold untill the sun comes up. I will be down to see you as soon as I can get a ride there and back. I don't suppose your tires would stand the trip up here. Are they rationing gas yet? If you Don and the kids could come up I would like you to see the camp. No one could describe it to you, you will have to see it yourself. If you could come Sunday come by the way of Red Cliff it is 25 miles closer than by Leadville. I will arrange to meet you at the new water tanks. When you come to a little black schack with the name Loudermilk you turn up the hill. If you come by Leadville stay on the oil road and you will see the round cedar tanks on the hill. The dust bothers my throat but that's all. I will try to call you Friday nite if I can talk well enough to make you understand. I hope you will have this letter by that time.

 I am well hope you are the same. Love to you and all from Hank. Room 104 Vandome Hotel Leadville Colorado c/o H.E. Bergland

Friday
Oct 9—42

Dear wife and family,

 I got your last letter yesterday. I am not inthused about the baby but how is Doris getting along? When does Don have to leave for the Army? I may be stuck here for another full week. I am sending $75.00. I will have to get another meal ticket tomorrow. If I leave here the middle of the week I can get refund on the rest of the ticket. If I can get a ride I may be down some nite but don't expect me. I guess I wouldn't see you before mid nite, if you are working the swing shift. I hear roomers here that a man is elligable for the Army, regardless of age, if the wife is working.

Did you get the tires yet. Have you got the gas ration card yet. It seems I am missing all the family troubles. I have never seen Vale yet but I am not working in the camp. I am on the Pando to Climax road. One hammer man came back yesterday, the one that was sick also had barbers itch, He may not be back.

Well I don't know anything else to tell you or ask you so I will close for this time. Love me, Hank

Saturday morning
Oct 10/42

Dear Hank,

Snow on ground. Pretty cold. How is it with you? If word comes that Don does have to be inducted before you come back I know he will want to see you. He may figure some way to get up there, is there any way we could see you? One of the ladies here in Lakewood telephones her husband up there. I know I couldn't catch you but you could telephone down here in case of emergency. We are all well, Gerald's finger is much better. Don left word he goes to work at 12 today. I'll get him up soon. He is really good to baby. Bobby went to union meeting last night. He is on an excavator now.

Are you having trouble to read my writing? Mr. Westervelt came down Wednesday from there went back Thursday morning he is a carpenter, Ferguson wants to know if you've seen Johnny yet?

Well darling this is all I can think of till another time. Love me? Rose

This part darling I forgot to add in my letter. The morning you left Mrs. Wellman called and said she was going to be down at the bank, would it be easier for me so thought, had to pay rent any way and so I took your 40.00 and added 5 from car and got that paid which I feel relieved then I got the car together and had Don pay that. Maybe I'll get straightened out yet. Is it so that you have long hours to work? Take care of your self and come home safe. I'm just putting in time I don't want any other life but what you can give me. Love, Rose

Oct 12 -42

Dear Hank,
 Monday evening. Thank you again, it seems funny me receiving money for my keep and not sending you any. One more week and I will have to pay rent again and also hope to be out of debt to Ferguson.
 I talked to Johnny and Madge today. Ferguson says he's going back up and work when Johnny goes back. I told Johnny to look you up and stick by you so you would have a way of coming down. Bob is to be laid off Thursday and is to go back Monday morning to work for Broderick & Gordon.
 I looked for you all Sunday evening. Am still looking for you.
 I sent 2 shirts, 2 socks, 1 underwear. I kept 1 underwear down here for fear you came and you could be clean. I'll send it up. I received the money today but my the note!!! I don't know what else there was to say, but . I sure was glad to hear your voice. How much did it cost you?
 Doris's baby will be born by Friday. Don is in such terrible pain from tooth ache. He was to have two of them pulled today but dentist told him to come back next Monday. So I don't know how he can take another week of it.
 Baby is better again. You know I think she is more homesick than anyone realizes. If the radio plays soft or sad music she just cries and cries.
 Dorajean got two letters from Vale. He went to work. Don Reeves went to work too. Oliver Grey is up there he has been there a week. He is an engineer.
 The kids have sure gathered scrap, they have over 3 ton at Lakewood School.
 I don't write all the things that worry me and I'm only waiting till

we can live. I'm not buying anything till you come home with me. I don't want to, besides I don't have no time. We'll talk it over when you come.

I'll roll up this other suit of underwear and send tomorrow also aspergum for your throat. Mr. Roosevelt is speaking tonight.

Let me know anything you want and boy do I love to get your letters. Love me, Rose

P.S. Johnny moved Madge down if he goes back he will live in barracks. He's sure a likeable boy, isn't he?

Tuesday morning!! Mailman came early no letter from you today. Do take care of yourself honey. Come see me when you can. I got the money of course did I tell you? Love me, Rose

I'm sending the suit of underwear.

Tuesday
Oct 13—42

Dear wife and kids,

How are you getting along now. No I stay at the camp I haven't been out of it since I landed here.

The mail that is addressed to Bergland at Leadville is delivered to the barracks. I haven't seen Vale yet. I seen Judge Brisco the other day. He is time keeper for the carpenters. I got the cigs and candy yesterday and the clothes today. They are all fine thanks a lot. It rained all nite here and was nice untill noon today then it started raining again and turned to snow and snowed most all afternoon. The snow is about all gone to nite but it looks like it might storm again tonite. It isn't cold yet. I am sending my dirty clothes, don't try to wash them yourself, they are filthy. I don't know how much longer I will be here. I will write again Friday when I get my check. Yes, I still love you. You tell the kids hello and good nite.

Love to you all from Hank
Sunday morning

I didn't get here untill after 8 o'clock. We went about two blocks. Last nite some of the lights went out on the bus and we were there an hour and a half. We ran out of the snow before we got to Georgetown the sky cleared and it was almost as light as day we had no trouble on the road at all untill we got over the pass and started down. We didn't have any trouble then but there were two big freight trucks in the road, one was hanging over the bank and the other was blocking the road behind it. We was there an hour and a half moving the one truck out of the road so we could get by. No one was hurt in the trucks. I got my check and cashed it and got a meal ticket. The post office wasn't open it may be later in the day. My check was only $75.73 I will send you $64.00. I seen Allen this morning he said the job is folding up fast.

Hank

Oct—14- 42
Wednesday morning

Darling,
    4 weeks ago this morning at 7:00 o'clock was the last I saw you. How are you? No news yet, Don had to come home with his pain last night he can't stand the noise. He truly is bad. Doris is still waiting. I told Bob he's going to prove to me he can take care of Doris safely. I sure make him toe the mark. Baby is very thin but her color is coming back again. I got Gerald a pair of shoes you know he needed them or I wouldn't of spent the money they were $4.00. I priced the overshoes and they also were $4.00. I didn't get them. Olive comes next. She is out. I saw a darling coat at Community Store, $10.75 but I'm waiting till you look, I want to see what kind of pocket book I get from you.
    It froze down here last night so I know it is very cold up there now. I dread winter I have to get coal again real soon. I have not got baby's doll yet. I don't get downtown. But I'm going to get it. Dora Jean and baby are as much trouble as Vale and Bob were, and it is an everlasting eating.
    She says Vale still loves her. It's the queerest couple I ever saw. I don't know if Joe Riley wet up yet or not I haven't heard any farther about them.
    Did you hear how much Mrs. Sloan ate & canned out of my garden> He got a deer a week ago, she has canned and made mince meat,

comes over and tells us how good but never a taste of the darn stuff. Believe me I can freeze up on her.

Well honey I don't care what the outsiders are doing just so we stick. Write me when you want. I love you—Rosalie

Tuesday
Oct 22, 42

Dear wife and kids,

How are you all. Did the baby miss me. Has Don heard from the army yet. I was going to write you last nite but I was called out to work after I checked in at 5:30 I checked out again at 6 o'clock and worked untill 11 o'clock. 7 hours over time Monday 2 hrs over time Sunday 4 hrs Sat. 2 hrs Friday. We had to wait at the gate Wednesday 4 hrs. It was after midnite when we found a place to sleep. We were all day Thursday getting our badges and finger prints. We have to stand in line for meal tickets and for meals and everything we do. A good many got discouraged and left before they went to work. All of the drain layers left Monday. They complained about the living conditions, the grub and the pay. There will be some laborers reclassified this week for drain layers. I am doing that work now. There isn't any hammer work to do yet. I seen Bill Suttees Sunday he is a carpenter here. We are straightened out all right now. It is cold in the morning but warm when the sun comes up. I have to pay $10.71 per week for a meal ticket. But the over time will make a good check when I get it. Well I will write again soon. Yours truly, Hank

P.S. address letters
Henry V Kirby
Vandome Hotel
Leadville, Colo c/o H E Bergland. Then the mail will be delivered to the barrox.

Tuesday
Oct—27 42

Dear wife and family,

How are you getting along with your job. By now has Doris gone to the hospital yet. Did Vail get out Sunday. I haven't seen him here yet. How is the weather there it is nice here. But looks stormy to nite. There is a man that did work here but quit, he lives on Ogden Street but I don't know the number, but he has some 600-16 tires to sell. I don't know how much he wants for them, his phone no. is Race 0973, name Wallie Miller. He knows me if you want to find out about them. Tell him I found out about them at Pando. This job may not last longer than this week. I don't know what they are going to do then. I will be home as soon as they are done I am feeling good now I couldn't stand much work the first two days but made it ok today. I wont get a check Friday unless I get layed off or quit. If I work another week after this I will have two full checks coming. I forgot to put a T before the 955 on the barrocks number. If I hear anything new I will let you know. I will write again in a couple of days.

 Love from Hank
 Pando Colo
 Barracks T-955 c/o of Cat Shop

               Oct 27—42

Dear Hank,
 Still no baby! I washed and scrubbed Sunday and cooked all the meals, etc. There is a lot to tell on that subject but I'm too tired tonight to write unnecessary.
 The work at plant is steady, hard work, no slacking. (I saw you) I know you had trouble getting up there but Bob wont put himself out. And I wont ask it of him. This was Norman's day off so walked home from plant and was I in?
 Do you notice the paper I'm writing on? Don got me some writing paper I was sure surprised. He is the only one that ever gets me a gift and I love him for it.
 I will have him get hen feed tomorrow. I have to leave so early in morning this week but next week I can do more around here. Dora Jean is absolutely broke. She got her coat. Vale only left her with $18.00 out of $84.00 he had the rest spent.
 Baby watches every nite to see what I will bring her. I am getting

her a snow suit and Olly a pair of shoes when I get paid. Ferguson's bill is $64.00 the electric bill came to $24.75 water meter is to be read this week. The money and letter came ok. The stamps are in one of the old letters, because I put them in or else when you opened the letter they flew out. There weren't many and if I never lose more it would be fine. That man's name is Melvin Reeves. He likes it fine. Lot better than Remington. I sure am wore out tonight I don't know how I will be by end of week. It's a lot harder than U.P. but it is inside work, so I guess I can stand it. Take care of yourself come home if you feel sick. Come see me when you can. Love me. Rosalie

P.S. I wont have time in morning to add anything so nite I'll seal it up. Love, Rose

Oct 30—42

Dear Hank,

Tomorrow is Dan's birthday. I received your letter today, no, Doris hasn't gone to the hospital yet. I called the Dr. he said with the first child she could vary several weeks. I called race 0973 he will let Don know tomorrow at noon if he can get them and that the price would not be his setting. They belong to his in-laws. My job is very good for a woman and I like the check it is better than the Union Pacific money, but the work is harder. They are still short 2700 women. They hire them every day. I hope you can get work around here close even if it is the Arsenal, so we could live together cheaper. As long as my time is 8 hrs. I like to get the money. I haven't bought anything since you were here, to work in. Don took my prescription blank to our eye doctor, the plant will make them free. I sure do like my friend Mrs. Reeves. There is no nastiness, no dirty stories or cuss words used around there and if there is time for anything else I would sure like to see it. Mrs. Hudson came up today for her $2.50. We can't get eggs any more from Nora. Our chickens are sure growing. Don got one tire, Bob Sloan made the deal. Don said it is a dandy he paid $5.00. Bob Ashton found us some tires but we had to pay for all three and they wanted $30.00. Only one was any good the other two were worth 50 ct. We didn't get them, I was so darn mad. Baby can't wait till I get her shoes and snow suit.

Yes we got Vale off on Sunday they had Bob Ashton take them to bus line. Dora Jean got her new coat. She's sure looking for a bit of money out of his check this week. Bob Sloan feels like you do, gamble, etc.

How are you and your lower trouble too. Do you really feel better or are you telling me so to keep me from worrying. Johnny rides to work with Bob out to Arsenal. We had a major injury out at a our plant 8 days ago, but it is nothing to speak of in size to people. There isn't much to write. I will set my alarm and talk to Don tonight. I will leave word what you said about tires. We need tires and we really need inter tubes. Also we have to get straightened out on rides. Norman quit his job today and went home. I don't have any outsider now but Dora Jean. Dora Jean got her coat just like the brown plaid I showed you in Community Store, so as far as I'm concerned that one is out. It has turned cold here again tonight. Well Hank I miss you and I do hope you don't have to stay a way too long. And about gifts for me and not being able to do for me, just don't any of you stop and explain debts to me when you are telling me I ought to get something for my self when a thing is given to a person it is given. If I have to pay for my own gift naturally I'll be stingy with myself. I am all out of cold cream. My hands are sure a mess. Doris did the washing today so I wouldn't have to wash Sunday.

Well darling I love you very much or I wouldn't be doing what I do. I do hope you are alright. Love me, Rosalie Saturday

Oct 31-42

Dear wife and family,

How are you making out now? I know you are having a hell of a time without asking. I am sure sorry you had to walk home from the plant. I suppose Bob thought it was good for you. I wish you didn't have to work out. Is Doris still carrying. Did Don get his teeth finished up yet? I didn't get a check this week. I am still feeling good. I have worked the full week except 3 hrs Sunday. I have a full check coming but I wont get it untill next Friday unless I get released before then. No one can terminate now only on Thursday or Friday of each week. I don't know when I will get released and I don't like to quit. I would like to be home tonite. *I feel more alive than I ever have since I came up here. We had two nasty days this week snowed and blowed like a blizzard. We had to work in it because we had a ditch open under the railroad tracks and had to finish the job, but I still wouldn't trade places with you. It was cold today but it didn't snow. I feel for Don starting the Model T in this weather. They say the Buena Vista job has started but B&G didn't get it. I think they will turn us loose when we get done here. One of our gang came back today. He has been in Fitsimmons Hospital for three weeks. I haven't found Reeves yet. He may be to the other end of the camp. If I have to stay longer than next week I will try to get down there Friday nite.*

 Well I will write again soon. Love from Hank

Oct—31- 42

 Darling it is Saturday nite and I don't have to go back to work until 4 PM Monday. My I'm tired, and I have bumps of muscles, I got my safety shoes today. They are all right but just another type of shoe to break in. I was on my feet the entire 8 hrs today. Packing Bandoleers, that is the toughest job there. I rather like packing even if it is hard. Vern is out some place, I hope he doesn't get into devilment. Was supposed to be no begging to night but we sure have had a lot of it. The girls let the coffee be froze without a speck in the house, can't buy any now till ration books are out. Haven't heard anything from tires yet.

 Baby has had the time of her life we had a little party for kids to night and ghosts & jack-o-lanterns.

 Dora Jean has not heard from Vale since he left Sunday. She told Mrs. Sloan she was disgusted the way things were run here. I still have to fix meals when I get home and what a meal. Our coal is about gone, one more stoker full.

 Well, Honey I will close hope you are fine. Do you want me to send under wear, shirts and socks? Answer real soon if you do. I hate to have them stranded up there. I heard you got a storm up there. Well nite. Love me, Rosalie

 PS Doris' baby was born 5 o'clock this morning, Nov. 1st. 7 lbs. 7 oz. boy a lovely shaped baby and very good looking. She had a time, they cut her side ways so it would be a clean break. I stayed till after she came out of Ether. She feels better now I called up. It was nice of her to wait till my day off. I can sort of get things straightened out here. Doris said tell you hello. Well bye, Love Rosalie

Broad Street Methodist
Columbus, Ohio
Wed. Nov 4/1942

Dear Gerald;

 Thanks for your letter. It was grand to hear form you. I have many happy memories of being with you last summer. You are the best caddie I ever had.

 Barbara is a poor letter writer- You jump on her and tell her she should write her Dad once in a while. I have not heard from her since I was out there last July.

 I so much enjoyed knowing your family. I like all of them. They are splendid fine citizens—just my kind.

 Mr. Hartley wants to be remembered to you and to them.

 I hope maybe to come to Denver again next summer—If I do you are hired.

 Write again -
 Sincerely, James Thomas

Nov. 4—42

Dear Sweetie Pie,

 Your letter received and sure glad. I can work better now. Sure if it isn't too awful I wouldn't quit I would just wait till it ended. I'm just as glad Buena Vista is out as I really want you around where I am. And as long as I have to work the plant is fine. The men look worse than the women.

 Say I just missed mail man so I will take this down to Lakewood and mail. Don got his notice to report to army on the 14th of Nov. I am slow getting around today. How will I stand it. I don't know what he plans to do now.

 I started to tell you a lot of things and now it is blasted out of me.

We can take it. Well I went down Monday and got my pay check from railroad it was $24.84. I got baby snow suit and Olly a pair of shoes. Baby is taking my working very good. I really don't mind my work Hank it is real factory work. Never an idle moment. And Ferguson says I look better since I went over there. You have several cards calling you to work there. My the wind is blowing hard today. I won't get over to see Doris today. They haven't taken the packing out of her yet. She nearly bled to death before and after the baby came. She always did bleed with a cut or a tooth. Well honey I'll close and sure do think you are doing swell. Keep well and I'm here when you do come. I didn't vote yesterday I was too busy. The rabbit had babys. Well I will close. Love Rosalie

PS Say Hank Dorajean has never heard another word from Vale since she put him on the bus a week ago Sunday. Out of all he made up there he left her just $20.00 and she bought her coat, etc. He was paid I suppose last Friday. Love me

Nov. 6- 42

Dear Hank,

Your very nice letter received. I work better when I get one and you do write a nice letter. I'm so glad you are back to normal, you bet I haven't lost my feeling for you. I was so worried about you, you remember old man Kaestner who lost all power about 45 yrs.

By this time you know Doris has a lovely boy it resembles Don and has reddish brown hair. So far it is all Kirby.

Bob and I have been going round and round.

Barbara was out to eat lunch with Don yesterday. She says she feels right at home, but leaves us to wait on her.

Dora Jean heard from Vale, he is going to Mexico City next job. He sent her some money. We had already had the FBI man up there hunting him up. Mrs. Reeves turned out to be a willy in the plant. She had experience from her man. It is like all places, half work and the other half don't. Gosh I was exhausted last nite, couldn't wait 1/2 hour till Don got in, I flopped in bed. I've been cooking Don something every nite.

My shift changes to 12 midnite till 8 in morning starting Sunday nite. So far I have stood it pretty good they say the best part is to nite, pay nite.

The tires you mentioned were a wash out. Something funny about the lay out. Mrs. Wilkins son is selling Don some with inter tubes, we think, Saturday. Don has a very bad tooth. He thinks when he goes out for induction on 14th he gets to come home for 7 days afterwards.

Barbara is moping around. Don knows how I feel and I don't have to talk. The small boys are fine. Olly and Madelyn are fine.

Don has just come down for breakfast. I will get it for him, so take care of yourself honey and I do think you are making the biggest money on that job and from then on it will be smaller. Say do you know I can't lay off for a single day I'm in the army now. Love me Rose

Nov. 10—42

Dear Hank,

Your letter and money received thank you I paid on Ferguson. I shall be so very glad to move away somewhere. If there is any danger of you being put in Army, I quit!! What have they done to you any way I was not working then. I can't seem to get caught up no matter what I make. If I pay one bill another one gets twice as big, I have an idea that you wont be able to read the as I'm laying down. I can't sleep. Doris comes home Tuesday nite. Vale sent Dora Jean $75.00 He don't know now how long he will be there that he may be made to stay there till job is finished. When is Allen going from there? I can't hardly bare the thoughts of Bob coming back here but I don't think it is much longer till army gets him and Vale. You don't have to hurry home to fast on account of Don leaving as he has notice he has a week to come home after induction. I bought $21.00 worth of tires. No body you know, 1 gas ration, I have a batch of papers to sign, don't know anything about them. I have to go to a shower for Shirley 11th I haven't seen her since the 15th Sept. I think the more I live that the Kirby children are a demanding lot. I ride with Ellen Westervelt, she said she looked in where I was working at plant and she thought how could children have there mother work. I told her not to pity me. I 'I've always made my own living. I got baby a pair of shoes today. Dora Jean is banking her money. Bob and I got into a squabble over what she called his money. It was Doris' hospital bill and Dr. bill. I gave it to her yesterday. Barbara was here when I came home midnite Saturday to stay all night. I had to do for all Sunday morning. I had to do the washing Sunday too as I had to change shift and went back to work Sunday nite at midnite. I am not on grave yard. I did pretty good but I can't sleep to nite so I suppose I will have a time tonite.

Honey I was interrupted last nite, Ray Pearcey took a taxi and came out here to stay all nite, the big truck broke down that was bringing up the cattle. Well I got supper for him and I left for work.

Say just incidently I don't like Remington or anything about it. I know what the others mean now. And the wages are cheaper the railroad.

It is now 9 o'clock Tuesday morning. Well we found Norman. We are all glad. I'll have to buy something for Shirley's shower.

Do you need these clothes? I hope it is not too miserable up there for you. and when you get a new job that it will be in Arizona. I'm freezing all the time. We have to work in an open place off the warehouse.

I will have to close and get this mailed. I also have been very sick with cold, but am better today if I haven't got some more to add to it. Take care of yourself and come home to me when you can. I know how you feel and it is good money darn it. Well good bye toots. Love me Rosalie

Monday
Nov 9- 42

Dear wife and family,

I got your welcome letter tonite. A letter from you and the time to come when I can go home is about all I have to live for. Allen told us today that we had 5 more miles of road to build yet that hasn't even been started yet. I would like to take a day off and come home but Allen insists on me staying, as they are so short on Hammer men. There is only 2 of us now. One works in the camp and I work up in Eagle Canyon some gang. One hammer man, one compressor man and the powder man. It sure was hell up there this morning, high wind and wet snow, it was a regular blizzard. Had to work with my rain coat on. It looks like winter has realy hit Pando. Toomstone the powder man owns that little Mexican log house just behind the snow white cafe. He also has 5 acres over by rockrest with 2 bunk houses on it. He wants to sell for $800 but no water on it. I wasn't considering that just news. Have you heard any more about the road or Mr. Long? Let me know when Don has to go. When will Doris be home? What will Dorajean do if Vale goes to Mexico? I didn't understand what you ment about Mrs. Reeves. I am afraid you stuck your neck out when you got your social security card and went to work. I think you are stuck for the duration. We've lost our liberty. They can tell us both what to do. I can't quit here now. Glen Wilson had to get furlow just like soldiers have to do to leave camp. Well maybe things will be different someday. I will be home as soon as I can. Don't look for me till you see me. Does Madelin think I am gone for good? Well good nite, Love me from Hank

PS again did you get the money I sent? My next check should be close to $100 I got 4 1/2 hrs extra time one nite. Love me.

Nov-12-42

Dear Hank,

Your letter received sure glad to get it. I'm sorry you have to be on that job. Do take care of yourself. Are you well? I am better my cold nearly got the best of me. 2 more nites to go on grave yard. Don got another tooth out, dry socket like mine was had to be packed and a stitch taken he is down there now getting packing taken out. Doris is home and fine, the baby is a very sweet child. Dorajean is downtown shopping. We are having a time with Janet Mae. Kids are well. Vern is very decent. Madelyn is wondering, but you did come home once so she feels you will come again. I know how hard it is to have to be away from home. I sure am glad when my eight hours are up. I'm staying up till about 4 o'clock this afternoon as I'm taking care of Janet Mae and I want to see Don yet today. He quit his job yesterday. So far Hank I can quit my job any time I want. When you come home if you want I will quit it, gladly. I'll tell you more when I see you. We now can take you to

Pando if you wanted us to. My legs are not doing so well. I told you Paul was here, well the other nite Ray Pearcy came.

I don't think any thing is hard to consider, we will have to think something soon. No news of road. No word from Long. I really feel as long as baby is safe with Doris, I should work as we have to save something.

When Don comes I am going to have this letter and package mailed as I knew you needed clothes. I hope you got my letter by now telling you Don has a week after he goes out to Fort Logan. Do you think I have told you most of the news? I love you very much Hank but you know that. I want you to take care of your self and I can quit when ever I want and I'm sure I haven't put you in the draft. I want to be ready where ever you go next. I work in a shop where the big warehouse doors are open at all times. I wear Don's heavy sweaters. So you writing about that up there makes me shiver down my spine. I almost wish I was in Arizona. Shirley's shower isn't till the 18th of Nov.

Seems like there ought to be a lot more to write about than there is.

I will write again soon, I am always so glad to get your letter. Well I will get ready to go to bed it sure takes the stuffing out of a person. You watch your self Honey. Keep well and I know Allen likes you but take care of yourself. No we have never heard of Broderick & Gordon, yet. I really mean to take that money for my coat.

Well Bye Love me. Rosalie

Saturday
Nov 14-42

Dear wife and Family,

Did you get home ok? I had good luck, got here at 5:45 this morning. I feel good my voice cleared up before I got here. Didn't miss sleep today I only dozed a little on the buss. Allen went in Friday, the draft board called him. He hasn't got back yet. Our gang is sure getting small. Soldiers are getting more numerous. I don't know any thing more new to tell you. I will write again soon. Love me from Hank.

PS I got your letter with stamps tonite. Thanks My overall size is 32 waist, 30 length but no hurry.

Nov-19-42

Dear Hank,

 Whatever you do try and get down for Thanksgiving dinner. I have the day off, if you can come Wed. nite on bus, I'll meet you when you call. Let me know if you can and if you don't have time to write, telephone. Love Me, Rose

 PS I'm sending the overalls up there to nite, but Don has the car someplace.

Thursday
Nov 19-42

Dear wife and family,

 How are you making out now. I hope you are feeling better and the gang have gone. I was up to the gard house last nite they said you could get a pass on Sunday, that is vissitors day. I could meet you at the station if I new what time you would get here. If you leave there at midnite Saturday you will get here about 6 in the morning, but you wouldn't see any country. You will have to walk where ever you go after you get here. If Don is home Sunday why don't you drive up. I think Loveland Pass is as good as any of them unless you come through South Park and Buena Vista then to Leadville. That is the best of all but farther. They say that job has started. It is about half way between Buena Vista and Salida. I don't know when I will get away from here. Allen had to go in again Tuesday. He hasn't got back yet. I guess the Army is about to get him.

 My check will be one day short tomorrow, but the next one will be long. I got 7hrs exra time this week. I will be glad when I get on another job and take you out of that mess. There were two men came back here form Phoenix they said there were so many men there they couldn't all get work. You know they would swarm there for the winter. There are 22000 men working on the Kansas job. Well I will write again soon. Love me, from Hank

Friday
Nov 20-42

Dear wife and family,

 I got your last letter today. I wish you wouldn't keep telling me that you are illegal and you have to beg for every thing you get. You know dam well I am allways glad when you get any thing for yourself. I am just not the kind to buy things for you because I don't know how to choose and besides we are allways pinched to death for money and if there is a way to make you legal we will do it when I get out of here. You know I don't begrudge you any money spent on you. What burns me up is you going without so much and doing so much for others. I know your legs are in bad shape and I hate to have you work at that dam plant. And you can quit any time. If you are working for your hospital bill, you may as well quit. There will allways be some one waiting for it and you will give it. I wish Dora Jean would get out and Doris and Bob would get there own home. Yes I will be home nite before Thanksgiving if I can get a ride with some body.

My check was $82 and 17 cts. I sent you $70.00 and got another meal ticket $10.71

I think most every one is going home for Thanksgiving. It started snowing this afternoon about 3 O'clock and is still snowing to beat hell. You don't have to tell me that I have the best of the deal. I know you have all the trouble and responsibility, but what can I do about it? You've always had that even when I was home. Well I will see you Wednesday nite. I wouldn't care if I get layed off for good. Well good nite. Love from Hank

Nov 22-42

Dear Hank,

If I don't write you to nite I'll feel low all day long tomorrow, but I am so hoping you get down for Thanksgiving as I am going to cook a turkey and have all the fixin's with candy and nuts.

Norman is back with us. His mother is just heart sick. She goes all to pieces. He is so very restless nothing very bad but just as tho there is no place for him. His mother gave me a turkey. I remember now last summer she said that if she raised any I had one for Thanksgiving, but I had forgot. It is now 10:00 can't seem to get kids to bed so I am leaving them up there. Don got Vern a game for his birthday. Present cost $4.00 but sure worth it for time being.

I have to get another ton of coal tomorrow. My I dread it. Two of our chickens were dead today, just too much cold. How are you and please Hank take care of yourself. That's all I ask of you up there. I don't know why I am such a darn fool about you, it ought to be out of me now after 25 years, but you are still tops. So do bring yourself home safe. Say, if you can stand that job up there, It isn't that I want you to quit. I hear others talk about their next jobs and they don't know where. Vale says Oliver Gray said if they stuck good there, their next may be Florida. Well you can tell me when you see me. A young woman in plant went yesterday to Arizona, Phoenix. Her husband got on down there. The name is Dymond. It's such a relief not to hear Janet Mae bawling. I took care of Doris's baby all afternoon so she could go with Bob. If I hadn't he would go any way. Well Honey I will see you Thanksgiving If it wasn't for Don I wouldn't ask you but I will put into this meal all of Xmas too.

Love me still, I love you, always will Rose

The house Rose and Hank lived in was already a hundred feet from the road, but the owners chose to have it torn down. This meant they had to find another place to live. It was unbelievable that the workers started tearing down the house while it was still occupied.

Just before Christmas in 1942, the family made their move to a little square frame house in Lakewood less than a block from Crown Hill Cemetery. It took several trips in the car to carry all the belongings, and there was no way for it all to fit in this little house.

One of the boarders, Norm Aronson, was not able to find a place to live so he came with the family. This meant that seven people were going to live in this two bedroom house. It had a partial basement where there was a monster of a coal burning furnace with a coal bin next to it, no windows and only a narrow stairway from the kitchen. The house was heated by one large grate in the hallway between the bedrooms. You had to step on it to get to the bedrooms. It was very hot, and you never wanted to step on it with barefeet. It left a waffle pattern on the bottom of your feet.

Rose and Hank had the large bedroom, and the three boys had the small bedroom. Ollie slept on the sofa and Madelyn's crib was in the livingroom. Madelyn had undulant fever from unpastuerized milk. She was in the crib a lot because of weakness.

There was no time to celebrate Christmas this year; it took some time just getting settled. Shirley gave birth to a boy, named Roderick Thomas.

There was a bathroom, but it was not hooked up to water. There was an out house behind the garage. If you wanted to take a bath, you heated water on the stove and dumped it into the bath tub.

There was a well in the back yard not too far from the septic tank. The younger children started getting sick and vomiting. The health department came out and tested the water from the well. It was highly contaminated from the drainage of the septic tank. Rose had to bring in bottled water and find out how long it would be before they could get city water hooked up.

The kitchen was small, barely room for two people at the same time and only had a little three burner gas stove.

Of all the houses they rented that were so large and roomy, this was the one they bought for thirty two hundred dollars. They didn't pay cash, the payment was fifty dollars a month.

The house was small, but it sat on seven tenths of an acre with water rights and an irrigation ditch running through it.

Don met a girl while in Cincinnati, Ohio, and they got married before he was sent overseas. Rose was not happy about this.

Doris had a baby boy before her husband, Bob Ashton, was sent overseas. She moved in with his sister, Marie, who had a baby the same age. They would share the house while their husbands were overseas.

Rose was still working at Remington Arms and Hank was going to have to find a job soon; her income was not enough to support the family.

It wasn't long until Hank found a job at Denver Steel and Iron Works under the viaduct on Colfax Avenue.

Norm Aronson found a job and was able to get an apartment and moved out of the house.

The house was very cold in the winter and everyone wanted to be close to the register to keep warm. The dining room was the closest to the heat, so everyone sat around the table. There was usually a jigsaw puzzle on the table to be worked. A table cloth was spread over the puzzle for meals. Since no one worked the same shift, they didn't all sit down to meals at the same time. Whoever got home first cooked dinner.

In the evenings after dinner, Hank and the kids would listen to the radio programs, *Captain Midnight, The Lone Ranger, I Love a Mystery, Can You top This?, and The Shadow* were their favorites. Rose was at work; she worked nights.

It became evident that the house was too small for the family, so Hank started digging out the other half of the basement. Shoveling it out a bucket at a time through the little window.

The front yard had a low place on half of it, so he dumped the dirt there to fill it in level with the rest of the yard. Every night when he got home he would dig so many buckets full, then fix supper. He was in bed by nine o'clock dead tired. He was up at five thirty to go to work.

Gerald and Vern would help haul the dirt when they weren't in school or working.

When the basement was half done, he decided it would need an outside entrance, so he and the boys started digging the area where the steps were to go. He had to cut through twelve inches of concrete foundation to make the door to the basement. It made it a little easier to dig out the rest of the room. Then he had to cut a doorway into the furnace room.

Shirley had given birth to a second child and brought him over to show the family. He was named Roderick Thomas Grunwald. Shirley mentioned to Rose that she needed her birth certificate. She had tried to get one, but for some reason she couldn't get it. They asked her a lot of questions that she didn't have the answers to. Rose told her she didn't need to have one. Shirley said she couldn't get her Social Security Card without it. They had a big argument and Shirley was very upset. She and her family left.

June 6, 1944, D-Day everyone was hoping the war was over and the men were coming home. Doris's husband came home and was a different person. He was abusive to her, and so she packed up and moved in with Rose and Hank.

The job at Remington Arms was over and Rose was out of a job. She heard about a restaurant that needed a cook, so she applied and got the job. They also needed a waitress so she got Doris a job there too. They went to work at three in the afternoon and got home at three in the morning. Rose had to close up the restaurant every night, and Doris stayed to help since they rode together.

Ollie was put in charge of watching Madelyn and Mike, Doris's son, while everyone was at work. She was eleven at the time. She had been taking care of Madelyn since the move to this new house. Rose slept during the day, and it was important that the kids were quiet and not disturb her sleep.

While the girls were in school, Michael had to go stay with a Mrs. Jones who took in children for working parents. Ollie would go by after school and pick him up and walk home with him. Madelyn went to a different school, so she rode the bus.

Don was out of the service now, and he and his wife, Barbara, had just had a baby boy, named Donald Dean II, they were living in Colorado Springs.

The house was pretty crowded, and Hank kept on working on it. The open stairway needed a cover to keep out the snow and rain. He put a door on it like a cellar for the time being. As soon as the weather warmed up, he would build a room over the stairway and add a sun porch, which would create more room next to the living room.

Rose wanted a new stove for the kitchen so she bought a new

electric stove that was twice as big as the little three burner. It sat in the living room in a wooden crate because the kitchen wasn't wired for two-twenty. That would have to wait.

There was a cast iron laundry tub in the corner of the kitchen with a wringer washer beside it that would have to be moved before the new stove could be installed. The laundry tub couldn't be moved until the basement was finished.

With Rose working nights and Hank working days, they didn't fight as much, unless it was on a Sunday. Many times when Rose came home at three in the morning they would get into it and the kids would cover their heads with their pillows so they couldn't hear the fighting. This went on until five thirty in the morning when Hank left for work.

With Vern and Geralds' help, Hank finally finished the basement and added on the step enclosure and sun porch. This was turned into a bedroom for the girls.

Vern was seventeen now and he could hardly wait to join the Army. So with a year to go to graduate, he enlisted and was sent to Fort Monmouth, New Jersey.

Not long after the basement was finished, Don lost his job and had to move in with Hank and Rose until he could get back on his feet. Their second child was just newborn when they moved in and Barbara's mother, Ernestine, came with them.

Doris, Michael, Madelyn and Ollie moved into the basement to make room for them. When spring came, the heavy rains made the irrigation ditch over flow and it flooded the basement. When the kids got out of bed, they were standing in one foot of water, some of the bedding had slid off the bed and got all wet.

Not long after Don and Barbara had moved in there was a big commotion in the living room early one morning. Doris ran upstairs to see what the matter was. The baby had suddenly died. Barbara was close to shock and her mother was beside herself with grief and pacing the floor raising her arms to the ceiling and wailing.

The coroner had to be called and with him came the sheriff's deputy. The younger children were confused about what had happened, but they stayed very quiet and out of the way. An investigation was made to see if they could determine why the baby died. Then the baby was taken to the morgue for an autopsy. These were very sad days for everyone.

A few days later the funeral was held for the baby at Fairmount Cemetery. The cause of death was an enlarged thymus gland that shut off air like suffocating.

Shortly after they buried their little girl, Don, Barbara and little Donnie moved to Aspen where they opened a western wear store. Ernestine went with them.

During their stay in Aspen Barbara gave birth to twins, but they were RH negative babies and had to be rushed to Denver for transfusions in the dead of winter. Thomas Ross and Kristen thrived after the treatment. Don got a job in Colorado Springs and they moved again. Not long after their move Catherine Marie made her appearance. Soon Don had an opportunity to move to Alaska. So the family packed up and had their mobile home towed to Anchorage.

***

Ollie was playing with the neighbor kids one day and their mother happened to mention that Shirley was her half-sister. Ollie was stunned to hear this and got upset. The mother apologized, she thought the kids knew.

Ollie knew better than to bring up this subject, so it would just have to be her secret until she could find out more.

Now that the basement was finished, Hank had to start digging a new septic tank. He put it on the side of the house where he had dumped all the dirt from the basement. It seemed like all Hank did since they moved in was shovel dirt.

Some how he managed to plant a garden on the other side of the irrigation ditch. Since they had water rights, he would have plenty of water for his garden. He seemed to enjoy walking behind the plow and working the soil. He always whistled under his breath while he worked. If you were near it sounded like *The Isle of Capri* and sometimes *Red River Valley*. When he wasn't working he liked to sit and whittle. He could take a match stick and carve it into a pair of pliers that opened and closed, all one piece. It was very fragile. He didn't make too many of the little ones, his favorite size was from a twig about two inches by one inch.

Hank suffered from a bad back and shoulder aches. He went to a chiropractor when the pain was too bad. He was told he had a crushed vertebrae and should have it operated on, but he would be laid up for six months while it healed. He decided he couldn't be off work that long flat on his back. It's a wonder he was able to dig out the basement and still go to work.

With Don and Vern writing about Army life, it didn't take Gerald long to decide he would enlist. He was seventeen and had a year to finish school, but he wanted to go now. He was sent to Fort Monmouth, New Jersey, where he got his diploma.

Doris and her son Michael found a house to rent, so they moved out. She was a saleslady for Wm. Dominick & Sons Auto Parts, she drove a black and red Model A Ford convertible furnished by the company.

Rose was still working nights and sometimes when she closed up the restaurant Sunday night, she would drive to Kit Carson to visit her sister Janet and drive back Monday since the restaurant was closed on Monday. Once in a while Hank and the girls would go with her.

Hank's brother Martin and his wife Evie would come to visit, and Rose did not give them much of a welcome. They were very nice, though. One time they came at the beginning of the school year and Ollie needed to go to Denver to buy books for her first year of high school. Uncle Martin offered to take her, and he even paid for the books. They liked all the kids, but they never had any of their own.

At least that is what everyone was told. But many years later when Aunt Evie died, she was buried next to her three babies that died soon after birth.

***

It had been a long while since Rose had heard from her brother Joseph, and much to her surprise, the day after her birthday, she received a letter from him.

March 26, 1949
Fort Worth, Texas

Dear Rose,

I have known for some time that you were not well, but I did not know you were so bad. If you would confide a little more it would be so much better. However, I guess we Reuters are all the same, when we really are in deep trouble we take our own counsel. I know I am that way. I have given some thought to you coming down here to recuperate away from all the tensions of home, but I wonder if you would be satisfied. If you think you would like to come and spend a month or so we would be happy to have you. We lead a pretty quiet life as a whole. This weather is some what warmer than up there too.

We are certainly sorry to hear about Don and Barbara's baby. It seems a shame that such things must happen. Are they spending the rest of the winter with you? I suppose Vern and Gerald are well satisfied in the services. I believe that is as good a place as any. I have never regretted my time spent there, but of course glad it is past.

We plan on going to Seattle in May. Will go by and see John and family on the way. Perhaps come back through Denver.

Write to me,
Rose. Love, Joe

Rose did not go to Texas to stay with her brother, but in May, Joseph and his wife Olga, stopped to visit on their return trip from Seattle. This was the first and only time that Rose's family had met Olga. She was a very pretty woman with a Texas drawl. Dark hair, dark eyes and fair skin.

***

Rose was surprised to get a long letter from Uncle Walter, with an update on the family.

Mikkalo, Oregon
February 2, 1950

Dear Niece Rosalie,
Ground hog day and the sun is shining brightly. Twenty below zero and about a foot of snow on the ground. Sounds like winter is still in the saddle, with no thought of changing its mind.
I got to thinking of you as the gay little girl I used to play with so many years ago, down at Sterling and at Sedro-Wooley. It may be that my little grand daughter, Linda Irene has stirred up the old memories. Auburn hair and pretty red cheeks, and full of fun, both of you.
The years roll around so quickly, and I am 76 now. My eyes and hearing are just as good as when you knew me, but my hair is snow white. However, I still feel quite young, and still do a fair days work when a carpenter job had to be done. Your Aunt Nellie is not very gray but she has to have a hearing aid; without it she hears very little.
Your Aunt Rosalie lives in Everett, and is not too well. The past three weeks she has been in the Everett General Hospital having had a sudden heart attack which pretty near took her away. A letter just to hand says that she is able to be up for five minutes a day now and is slowly gaining strength.
Uncle Ernest died in Sedro-Wooley shortly after the new year. He took pneumonia which with other complication caused him to pass away rather quickly. The two boys were at home with Aunt Lilah at the time. The weather was so bad that neither Rosalie or I could attend the funeral.
Lets see, you have three boys grown, and three girls, too. A good family and must been lots of fun and trouble, too. When we lived at

Sedro-Wooley we had a neighbor by the same name as your husband's—Kirby. Nice folks, as aristocracy goes. They had plenty of money.

The weather reports tell us that you folks in Denver are really good friends with king winter. You are so high in elevation that it must be hard to boil potatoes in a hurry. This year really cold.

We get a letter from your sister Janet every so often. They seem to be in a fairy belt where the bad storms do not give them bad times. Some day I am hoping to get an opportunity for a few days in your State. But when, now that I am called old.

Since coming back to America in 1940, we have been pretty busy most of the time. I taught in the Caldwell Academy, near the capital city Boise for one year, and then went to Glendale, California, and was working with the Voice of Prophecy for four years. The past few years I have been here on the farm with our son-in-law, building them a good home, and other work that a carpenter only knows how to do.

If you have a radio, I am sure that you must have heard the Voice of Prophecy broadcast. They have one of the best quartets in America. This Broadcast with near 700 stations is now heard in every country on earth. And they have free Bible correspondence schools in many languages. I enjoyed that work, but having to sit at a desk everyday was not good for my heart.

I know that I have not been a very good correspondent, when since we were such good friends long ago you would naturally have expected me to write at least once a year. Please forgive the failure and write me.

With love and best wishes from your Uncle Walter and Aunt Nellie.

Uncle Walter Gillis went to Korea in 1934 to set up the largest printing office in Europe and preached as a missionary. When he came back to the states he worked as an instructor on the VOICE OF PROPHECY PROGRAM on the radio, was still on it May 6th at the age of 72.

CHAPTER 11

EMPTY NEST 1950

Shirley and Bob came by to visit and told Rose and Hank that they had found a farm in Delta. They had sold their place in Westwood and were all packed up and ready to move.

Their kids could have a sheep to raise for 4H, and they would have chickens and pigs and raise their feed. Shirley could have a vegetable garden and lots of flowers. The house was a large two story farm house, but there was no running water. They would have to carry water from the well. The house had a perfect room for a bathroom, but it was empty.

Shirley tried one more time to get Rose to tell her who her father was and all she would say was, "All you need to know is his name, Frank Moore."

Shirley and her family left the next day. She could never stand up to her mother to get anything resolved. She wrote from time to time, but visits were rare. She never forgot any of her sister's and brother's birthdays. Without fail a card or a small gift would arrive a day or two before the birthday.

Rose was not good about writing to her brothers and sisters to keep them up to date, but they wrote more often. Just before Thanksgiving a letter arrived from her Brother John.

October 3, 1951
Burbank, California

Dear Rose and all,
So glad to have your letter. Noticed yesterday, in the paper, where

around fifteen hundred veterans had returned from Korea in Seattle. Just wondered if Vern was among them. I know it is wonderful to get him out of there and sure hope Gerald gets home real soon too. I know Vern is happy about his new promotion to Sergeant. He surely will be able to stay in the States now.

Chuck is stationed at Nuremberg, Germany. It is about five miles out of Munich. We hear from him about every week. Takes a letter from five to seven days. He just went to work a couple of weeks ago. Had to wait for clearance papers to get through. He expects to be at this place three years. It seems like a long time, but guess the time will go pretty fast. He will spend his twenty-first birthday there. John spent his twenty-first birthday in Germany, too. Quite a coincidence.

He says the food and quarters are very good and he can't think of anything he'd want, he can't get there, so guess we have a lot to be thankful for. He didn't get his eye taken care of yet. He had checked about it and they'd told him to report any Tuesday or Thursday and they'd take him to the hospital and have it taken care of. right after that he went to work, so the last letter said he thought he'd wait awhile.

John is working swing shift now, at Lockheed, for a couple of months. I sure get lonesome in the evenings. He goes to work at four in the afternoon and works until twelve thirty in the morning. Of course I have to go to bed so I can get up and go to work in the mornings. One good thing about it, he is getting to watch the World Series on television.

Olga and her brother stayed all night with us a couple of weeks ago. Joe didn't come along. He hadn't been feeling too good. Olga's brother was on his vacation, so she came along with him. They had visited Spratt's children in San Diego and a brother here in Los Angeles. They were driving the Cadillac.

Hope you get to visit Janet. Haven't heard from her for a while. Hope she is feeling OK.

Well, take care of yourselves folks. Let us know if Vern gets home OK and how Gerald is getting along.

Love to all, Malissa and John

Ollie graduated from high school and married her sweetheart who was in the navy. They moved to San Diego while his ship was in dock.

Madelyn didn't like being the only one home, so when Uncle John and Malissa came to visit that summer she begged them to take her back to California with them. They thought that would be a good idea and why not stop in Delta and take Linnette with them, since they are so close to the same age.

Madelyn wasn't too happy with that arrangement, but she was so eager to go she wasn't about to cause trouble. The trip to California was fun. Uncle John showed them all the sights and would stop for snacks. He always had funny stories to tell.

Rose and Hank were alone. For the first time in their lives they had the house to themselves. Rose worked nights and Hank worked days. Nothing really changed.

Uncle John was full of energy, he enjoyed having the girls spend the summer, and he did all the cooking. Malissa had a job too, and John was devoted to her. He worked at Lockheed, and on his days off he showed the girls Burbank. Almost every Sunday, friends and relatives that lived within fifty miles came to visit and John cooked for them all. It was nothing for him to cook for twenty people who dropped in.

John Reuter was the catalyst that kept the brother and sisters in touch. He was so happy when their sister Ruth found them when she was twenty-one and married to Edward Stowe. He was the only one that made an effort to visit them frequently.

Fort Worth, Texas
8/14/52

Dear Rose and Hank,
    A line to let you know we are still here and for the present at least still together. I have been sick all summer, but feel some better now.
    We really enjoyed our visit up there this summer. John and I did some rabbit hunting down at the ranch. 1st time since I was a kid.
    Also had a nice trip to S.D.

Certainly hope all of you are doing OK. And how did Madeline like Calif.?
Hope to get up that way again before too long.
Write!!!

Love, Joe & Olga

Their brother Joe was living in Fort Worth, Texas. A retired Army Major, now an agent for Lincoln Life Insurance. Married to Olga, no children. He had been missing, no one knew where he was, his entire tour of duty.

5 Mar. 53

Dear John & Malissa,
Well they have finally decided to operate—and now are merely waiting for a bed in the surgical ward. Don't know just when that will be, but perhaps they will cut at me about next Tuesday. The consensus of opinion of twelve doctors is they don't know what to do except cut in and see what the main trouble is—they can't agree just why I do not get better from medical treatment. Actually I am not too "sold" on the operation, but I feel I must trust their judgment.
Olga came back down yesterday and will stay awhile. Got a letter from Ruth and of course hear from Janet regularly. I do not feel too low in spirits, but I do wish they could give me more definite hope of a cure, they are so cagey.

Love, Joe and Olga

They only had a short time to catch up on his life, he died of throat cancer when he was only fifty-two.

***

Madelyn came home the end of summer, in time to go to school. Ollie returned about the same time; she would live at home while her husband's ship was out to sea for ten months.

Ollie got a job with the telephone company, but only worked for six weeks. It turned out she was pregnant and was hemorrhaging, if she didn't go to the hospital she would lose the baby. She was confined to her bed the rest of the pregnancy with intermittent trips to the hospital. After seven months the baby had to be taken by c-section. The baby weighed two pounds, nine ounces. She had to stay in an incubator for two months. She was named Cynthia Jeanne.

Ollie's husband Chuck came home soon after the baby was allowed to come home. It took weeks to notify him he was a father.

They packed up the baby and returned to San Diego. Instead of living in Naval Housing, they found a house to share with another Navy wife whose husband was a Chief Warrant Officer. He was rarely home, so she liked the company and she had a little girl named Cynthia also and a little boy named Bruce. This house was on Point Loma which was close to the beaches. It sat up high on the Point and you could look out over the bay and see all the ships coming in.

Their time together was short, as Chuck would be shipping out again and Ollie would go home for another ten months. Seven months later Ginger Marie was born by c-section, she weighed four pounds. This time they got word to Chuck so he could be home for her birth. Then they packed up both babies and returned to San Diego.

In 1954 Chuck was discharged from the navy and they packed up the babies and went to visit Chuck's grandmother and grandfather in Yucaipa, California. While there, his grandmother had a severe heart attack and died. His grandfather made arrangements to have her body taken to Colorado for burial. Aunt Amy and Uncle Rex accompanied everyone to Denver.

Chuck and Ollie moved to Golden and soon after they had another baby, born by c-section, they named her Marci Lea.

By this time Gerald and Betty had two daughters close to the same age as Ollie's and in November of 1956 they had their third daughter; all born by c-section. Their girls were Janet Rose, Nancy Ellen and Candy Jean.

Vern was working in Seattle for Boeing Co. He and his wife Freddie had two children Lynette, and Larry was four years younger.

CHAPTER 12

1960

Rose was making more trips to Kit Carson now to see her sister Janet. Hank was having more pain in his back so he was spending more time at the chiropractor's.

Madelyn was busy with school. She and her friends got involved with KIMN radio station and did some modeling around Denver. One time she was advertising for Hot Point Appliances and paraded around Sixteenth Street dressed as a red devil. Then her friend was voted MISS KIMN and Madelyn was the runner up. They did promotions and had to ride on the back of a motorcycle to Cheyenne Frontier Days.

Madelyn was about to graduate and she decided she wanted to go to beautician school in California and live with Uncle John and Aunt Malissa. They thought that was a grand idea.

When Madelyn arrived in California, her cousin Chuck was home from the service. She had not seen much of him when she was growing up, so it was a chance to get to know him. He was planning on going to the university after a few weeks of vacation.

Madelyn was happy going to school and she liked learning all the hair styles and make-up techniques. Chuck took her to all the fun places around Hollywood and the beaches, she couldn't ask for a better escort. John and Malissa enjoyed having her live with them, she was like a daughter to them.

She and her cousin Chuck had become great companions and soon turned into a romance.

Rose went to California for the wedding, but Hank refused to go. Rose didn't approve of Madelyn's wedding dress, so she took her shopping and selected the dress she thought was appropriate.

Rose and Hank settled into their new lifestyle with Rose still working nights and Hank working days. Rose drove to Kit Carson at least once a week now. Janet was not well and she was in and out of the hospital in Cheyenne Wells, close to the Kansas border.

At the age of sixty-five Anna Janet Reuter McKeever died of cancer. The oldest of the six orphans. Her brothers, Charles and Joseph had preceded her in death. Now there were only three of the orphans living.

Janet and Ira had many friends in Kit Carson and surrounding towns. They had stuck it out and survived the hardships of living on the prairie like the Ramseys, Meiers, Thompsons, Collins, Wherrys, Sweitzers and the other homesteaders that raised their children, made a good living, and sent many of them out to make a better life than they had. But many of the children had fond memories of their childhood.

Rose and Hank started taking a few trips now that they were in a better financial shape. They stopped in Delta to visit Shirley and her family, then went to California to visit her brother John and his wife Malissa; their daughter Madelyn, husband Chuck and their baby son named Joseph James. From there they went to Seattle to visit their son Vern and his family. They never went to Illinois to visit her sister Ruth and her family. They only kept in touch by letters.

About the time Rose and Hank were thinking about retiring, Rose had a very serious automobile accident which put her in the hospital for a couple weeks. She went home to recuperate and Hank was fixing the meals and waiting on her when he wasn't at work. It was May when Rose was able to be up and around and do things for herself. Hank was getting the garden plowed to plant his vegetables when he collapsed in the field and died instantly of a coronary occlusion.

Rose commented that very few of the World War I veterans were expected to live to collect their retirement because of the mustard gas used during the war in Europe.

He was entitled to be buried at Fort Logan Military Cemetery, but Rose chose to have him buried at Crown Hill Cemetery.

Shortly after Hank died, Shirley and Bob sold their place in Delta and retired in Texas.

Rose continued working. She was highly respected by everyone she worked for. She was now working at the Jefferson County Bank, as a cook for the employees. The Bank had remodeled and installed a complete kitchen in the basement in order for her to prepare the hot meals for their lunch. She no longer worked nights.

Each year she was given vacation time and she now was able to travel. She would fly to Alaska to visit her son Don and his family and stop in Seattle to visit her son Vern and his family.

Rose went to visit her brother John, in California. He was thinking of retiring from Lockheed, where he had worked for many years. He was not feeling well and couldn't keep up the pace. Shortly after Rose's visit, John died of stomach cancer. He was 73. Now there was only Ruth and Rose left of the orphans.

January 16, 1973
Marysville, Wash.

Dear Ruthie,

I don't expect you to remember me only from what you have been told. I am your uncle Laurence's wife, your Aunt Myrtle. Your brother John thought it would be a good idea for me to write you so here I am. He gave me your address over the phone and I hope I got it right. I used to write to your sister Rosalie but lost her address some way and haven't written for a long time. So I am hoping you can send it to me again.

You were just a baby about 2 years old the last time I saw you. Do you remember anything about Three Lakes at all? There is nothing left of it now at all. Three Lakes was quite a busy place in 1905 and 1906, when we were there. We worked in the mill boarding house for nearly a year. After about 40 years we went back just to see what it was like and it was all gone.

We had a surprise visit from John and Malissa several years ago and Rosalie was with them. We were so surprised and happy about it all that I didn't realize what it was all about until they were gone. Wish you could have been with them to. Does Rosalie live very far from you? Uncle Laurence will be 89 his next B.D. and I will be 84 next month. We don't have a car any more so we stay pretty close to home most of the time. Laurence goes bowling 4 or 5 times a week when he can find some one to take him. I don't like bowling so I stay home and piece quilts, crochet rugs, and afghans when there's nothing else to do. Our winter started early this year, have had 2 very stormy spells, with snow and ice, but it is raining tonite. Hope this finds you well, I'm looking forward to hearing from you soon. With love from Aunt Myrtle

Rose was not adapting to living alone, so she had Doris move in with her. Doris's son Mike was in the service and stationed in New Jersey. Doris had a job in Denver so she was home in the evenings.

By now, Rose had several grandchildren and the family dinners, usually on the holidays, were held at her house.

The house that Hank had spent so many weeks hauling dirt out of the basement, was now becoming a liability, the upkeep was more than Rose could handle by herself. Winters were hard and some one had to plow out her driveway for her to get to work. It was time to sell and find an apartment that was convenient for her.

Rose had lived in the house for thirty years, the longest she had been anywhere. It was not easy to give up the house and move from this neighborhood.

Rose finally made the move to an apartment where the walks were shoveled and the yards were kept neat and trimmed.

She was getting up in years now, and the work was getting harder, so the Bank did another remodel and all she had to do was keep the food fresh that the employees could heat up in the microwave. She had been there twenty five years cooking their lunch every day.

Her apartment was a tri-level and one night she fell over the railing into the lowest level and laid there until the next afternoon when her granddaughter came to visit her and the mailman was there and they both were surprised that the door was still locked. The apartment manager was called, and they found her laying at the bottom of the steps. She was taken to the hospital and found that she had broken both wrists and her pelvic bone.

While she was in the hospital, her children moved her to another apartment, in the same complex, without any steps.

After a month in the hospital she was giving the doctors fits and wanted out. She could not go home until she was able to get around by herself, she would have to go to a nursing home for rehabilitation. She went, but she would not co-operate with her therapy. She ordered her children to get her out of there. After three weeks she went home, but she would have to rely on a wheel chair. She was not ready to accept that she could not live alone, but she agreed to let Gerald and his wife Betty moved in with her.

She refused to use the wheel chair and had to relent and use the help of a walker. Needless to say she retired from her job after this incident. She was eighty-four.

She fully recovered from her injuries and was able to get around without the aid of the walker. Gerald and his wife had been with her for two years and it was time for them to move out. It was not easy living with her; she could be very unpleasant.

Since she had given up her car before the accident, she had to rely on family and friends to take her shopping for groceries and other items she needed. A friend that cleaned for other tenants in the complex, agreed to add her to the list of clients and would clean the apartment once a week for her.

She lived in this location for six years and then decided to move to California to be closer to her daughter Madelyn, who was now divorced. Madelyn had a small apartment that was vacant at the time, and Rose had all her furniture shipped to California and moved in. Madelyn had three units and lived in one of them and rented out the others, so Rose was just a few feet from the other units. After a month it was obvious that this arrangement was not going to work.

Rose assumed that her daughter was lonely and in need of company, so she would watch for her to come home after work and expect her to spend the rest of the evening playing cards, eating and drinking coffee.

Madelyn had tried to get her to take the shuttle bus that was provided by the Senior Resource Center to take senior citizens any where they needed to go, whether it was shopping, the doctor, to see a play or dining out. This idea did not go over well with Rose. She was insulted that Madelyn thought she was a *Senior Citizen*.

She did not move to California to spend time with strangers. Madelyn had a life, and she wasn't going to change it to suit her mother. Rose called her daughter in Colorado and told her to find her an apartment. Right now, she was catching the next plane and shipping her furniture.

Ollie got busy and located an apartment in Lakewood that was ready for Rose to move into immediately. It turned out that one of her school chums mother had several units and one was vacant. She knew Rose from years back so there was no trouble renting to her.

Rose and Mrs. Johnson would have coffee together from time to time and talk about the people they both knew when Lakewood was a small town. When Rose visited with her friends she always made up things that sounded more interesting. She always wished her life could have been more exciting and wealthier.

After about three years Rose had some funny episodes, like carrying the trash to the street in the dead of winter on an icy driveway, fainting in the kitchen and keeping the curtains closed all day to look like she wasn't out of bed yet. She was ninety three now and probably shouldn't be living alone. So she moved into a basement apartment at Ollie's house. She could have her own kitchen, bathroom and private entrance, but some one was close at hand when she had a problem.

During the time she lived in this apartment her son Don had retired in Alaska and moved to Canada and built some houses on land that his son owned. He seemed to go down hill pretty fast and one of his sons called to tell us that if we wanted to see him alive, we should come visit him before he got any worse. Rose was in no condition to travel that far and Doris didn't want to see him if he was that sick. So Madelyn and Ollie flew to Canada to spend a few days with him.

Three months after their visit he died of pancreatic cancer. He was buried on a Sacred Indian Burial Ground in Lac La Biche, Canada. He was a friend to the Indian Tribe and helped them build housing for their school and community gatherings. His son was a teacher and principal in their school. They honored him by allowing him to be buried on their sacred ground. He was sixty eight.

That same year Ruth's family notified Rose that Ruth had quietly passed away, after a bout with a liver tumor. Now her baby sister was gone and Rose was the lone survivor.

Looking back, now it seems so strange that four of the children died of the same illness that killed their father.

Lombard, IL
Feb. 12, 1989

Dear Aunt Rosalie,
I have been thinking about you and know there must be things you want to know about your dear baby sister! I will try to tell you many things, some that words can't tell!

Despite the long separations all you Reuter children had, Ruth always held you close. During the three months she was with us she had time to share with me many memories and stories as well as feelings of family. She felt fortunate in every way. She had two loving families and returned that love many times over, often through hard work—singing and humming her way through tough times as well as the good.

She told me you and Janet named her—and such a beautiful name, of which she was proud, always using the "N" for Naomi as well as the Ruth! She recalled your days at the orphanage, your being one of the "big girls" and her memory of your little favors or kindness' to your baby sister. She surely got her keen sense of family love from her early years with you and Janet.

At her memorial service her pastor said "She loved her church, her family, her garden and God." The Altar Guild, members young and not-so-young treasured her as a person and also for her knowledge of how to-do-it "RIGHT"!

On Christmas Eve we made the trip to Fred's house where she and Edward usually went. Many of the grandchildren were there, along with various cats and dogs! Ruth was definitely NOT the little old lady in the corner! Although somewhat tired and weak, she chatted with everyone, and thoroughly enjoyed the little ones who would plop up on her lap or beside her for a few minutes, then run off, soon to be back with a "goodie" to share! It was a good time for all—but at some time for each of us came the knowledge it was truly our last Christmas together.

From early November until she died, January 26, she was with us—first because of the care needed after her cataract surgery—then, as we lived together we could see her strength was very low. She slept a lot and ran out of breath and energy quickly—3 or 4 minutes on her feet was exhausting. So, against her hopes, she never went back home. She wished it otherwise but slowly could see some advantages to being here— No cooking—and she did eat well—no stairs—no house cleaning (although Ned's "neatness" tendencies got to her- he'd "make her tired" just watching him clean!) and she found a favorite spot to sit and crochet (a blanket for the next great grandchild as yet unborn).

We have a "sun room" which adjoins her room and bathroom, carpeted full of plants (some of her beloved violets included), with floor to ceiling wall-to-wall south facing windows. She napped in the sunshine and woke to watch the squirrels cavorting in the leaves, grass or snow.

Her liver- tumors, I suppose kept growing bigger so that clothing was uncomfortable—She vowed she was eating too much- but welcomed an elastic drawstring skirt I made for her—with pockets, which especially pleased her. We had a few discussions about dressing or not dressing—She insisted on wearing pantyhose and shoes if there was any chance a visitor might come—even the nurse! To get dressed—and bathe- took all her strength—but she insisted on doing it all by herself even though we could have a Hospice health aide to help her. She would say "we'll see—not yet, dear!"

Throughout the entire time she had very little pain. The strongest medicine she took was extra strength Tylenol until the very last day.

Bertha and Sandy came January 16th and stayed for ten days. They had a wonderful visit. She loved being read to and Bert loved reading. They got used to each others' schedules of rest and awake and used the time they had well. The night before they were to leave it was agreed they would not wake Ruth in the morning—an early flight. So on Wednesday they said their good -byes and Ned took them to the airport about 6 a.m. When Ruth awoke, she went to the bathroom by herself, put her teeth in (she always felt "naked" without them!) but was too exhausted to get back to bed so she just stopped and sat down on her favorite couch on the way back.

I brought her breakfast there, as I sometimes did, and she ate every bit, taking her time. While she was there, Ned and I decided to dust and vacuum her room—I changed her bed, moved her plants around, dusted , etc. all the time watching and talking to her. She seemed nervous and apprehensive which was not like her. By the time she got back in bed, Ned was concerned enough about the nervousness and breathing difficulty to call the hospice nurse who came very soon, got some medicine to calm her down (a tranquilizer) and started her on an oxygen machine which she had brought. She also inserted a catheter so Ruth wouldn't worry about a bed accident. During all this it was hard to understand but each of us (Ned, the nurse, and I) all understood her to say what a wonderful visit she'd had with Bertha- "that's all I needed" which we took to mean she was ready. We were not alarmed but concerned enough to let the family know where was a change. All she took that day (after breakfast) was water- every time—her same old self- saying "Thank you , dear"

At 8 p.m. Bob, Delia and Maria came- They hadn't been able to see her since before Christmas—she spoke to each of them, even remembering Maria had just had her 21st birthday! About 10:15 she told Maria "You don't have to stay, I'm very tired and need to rest" So Maria left and came to be with the rest of us in the livingroom.

The next person to go in found her sleeping peacefully and then when Ned went in at 10:35 p.m. she had died, very peacefully. While Ned called Hospice nurse, the rest of us said a prayer, and cried over a beautiful life, lovingly lived, which had left us.

Sometimes, looking back, one would have changed things. We don't feel that way. If we could choose it was a good way to go. Ruth knew who got her household things and was pleased to learn of each "thing" given to a family member. She even knew who is buying the house and was delighted, "They'll make my garden even better!" she said.

For me, I treasure the near 40 years I've know this wonderful, simple, in some ways always childlike lady. I learned from her about motherhood, grandmotherhood, and how to be a good mother-in-law (at least I hope some of her example rubbed off!) I learned about flowers and gardening and canning. I learned about rummage sales and generosity—of accepting family because they are and not expecting what they aren't. From her I learned of duty and unquestioning loyalty (but I don't come close to doing!) to family and church.

Well dear, you are probably exhausted from this (I pity the poor soul who has had to read this to you if you can't make it out yourself!) I am enclosing one of the service programs and a hankie I found in her pocket—R for Ruth and Rosalie! Love, Mary

A year later Doris died of a gastric hemorrhage. One night her husband heard a noise in the bathroom, and he found her on the floor in a pool of blood. It was on her seventieth birthday.

Soon after Don and Doris died, Shirley had a stroke and couldn't talk, she was in a nursing home in a wheel chair. A couple of years before she had been diagnosed with diabetes. The last time they came to visit, she had tried to get Rose to tell her more about who her father was. If she had known anything about him she might have been forewarned if she would inherit this disease. None of Hanks children had diabetes and no one on his side of the family had it. There was no history of diabetes on Rose's side of the family either, so it had to come from her unknown father.

She had passed the tendency of this disease on to her two children and they, onto theirs.

Rose would tell her nothing. Two years later Shirley died never knowing the circumstances of her birth.

Rose is now a hundred and one, living in a nursing home for the past year. Her mind is alert, but the body is failing. She is the last of the six orphans. She has out lived anyone who would know anything about her past.

October 7, 1998, Rosalie passed away. *The Isle of Capri* and *The Red River Valley* were played at her funeral.